Grammar, Usage,
and Mechanics Workbook

Language
Network

McDougal Littell
A HOUGHTON MIFFLIN COMPANY
Evanston, Illinois • Boston • Dallas

ISBN 0-618-05261-5

9 10 11 12 13 14 15 16 – VEI – 09 08 07 06 05 04 03

Contents

Special Features

The *Grammar, Usage, and Mechanics Workbook* contains a wealth of skill-building exercises.

Worksheets correspond to lessons in the Pupil's Edition.

Each page focuses on one topic or skill. A brief instructional summary on the **Reteaching** page is followed by reinforcement activities.

Key words and phrases are highlighted for greater clarity and ease of use.

When appropriate, example sentences demonstrate how to complete exercises.

Each lesson has different levels of worksheets. **Reteaching** introduces the skill; **More Practice** and **Application** extend the skill with advanced exercises.

Tabs make it easy to navigate the book.

Each page clearly refers to its corresponding part in the Pupil's Edition for easy reference.

Name _____   Date ____

Lesson 1

Prepositional Phrases

Reteaching

A **prepositional phrase** consists of a preposition, its object, and any modifiers of the object.

> Scientists observe stars <u>through a telescope</u>. (The preposition is *through*.)

An **adverb phrase** modifies a verb, an adjective, or another adverb.

> We see many stars <u>with the naked eye</u>. (The phrase modifies *see*, telling how.)

An **adjective phrase** modifies a noun or a pronoun.

> Light <u>from the stars</u> travels quickly. (The phrase modifies *light*, telling what kind.)

A. Identifying Prepositional Phrases

Underline the prepositional phrases in the following sentences.

> **EXAMPLE** Astronomers have made many discoveries <u>about the galaxy</u>.

1. Can anyone count the stars in the Milky Way?
2. The Milky Way looks beautiful on a clear night.
3. I enjoy stargazing from a nearby hilltop.
4. Clusters of stars form constellations.
5. Seven very bright stars surrounded by dust form the Seven Sisters.
6. Stars emit huge amounts of light.
7. Starlight passing through the atmosphere produces twinkling.
8. Stars change size, shape, and color in their life spans.
9. Different stars are fascinating to astronomers.
10. For centuries, people have looked into the heavens.

B. Identifying Words Modified by Prepositional Phrases

Underline the prepositional phrase in each of the following sentences once. Underline the word it modifies twice.

> **EXAMPLE** The quarterback <u>threw</u> the ball <u>into the end zone</u>.

1. Can you pronounce the name of the country?
2. The soprano sang one of my favorite songs.
3. In the cave an ancient artist had painted a hunting scene.
4. Along the path we planted pink and yellow tulips.
5. Can you see well in the dark?
6. The baseball flew over the fence.
7. Can you see that mountain in the distance?
8. The band played a song from a popular musical.
9. One of the hockey players was seriously injured.
10. During the storm all traffic stopped.

CHAPTER 3

For use with Pupil's Edition pp. 66–68

GRAMMAR, USAGE, AND MECHANICS WORKBOOK   **49**

Name _____ Date _____

Nouns

Reteaching

A **noun** is a word that names a person, place, thing, or idea.

Type of noun	Definition	Example
common noun	general name for a person, place, thing, or idea	monster
proper noun	name of a particular person, place, thing, or idea	Big Foot
concrete noun	name of something perceived by the senses	fur
abstract noun	name of an idea, quality, or state	fear
singular noun	one person, place, thing, or idea	photograph
plural noun	more than one person, place, thing, or idea	cameras
collective noun	name of a group of people or things	herd
compound noun	single noun formed from two or more words	footprint
possessive noun	noun that shows ownership or relationship	hiker's boots

A. Finding Nouns

Underline every noun in each sentence.

1. Of all the world's monsters, the dragon is best known.
2. Ancient cultures imagined the dragon as a giant snake.
3. During the Middle Ages, dragons were depicted with wings and legs, breathing fire.
4. Dragons resemble lizards in the artwork of earlier cultures.
5. Roman mythology tells the story of Hydra, a nine-headed dragon.
6. For centuries, Scotland has claimed the monster of Loch Ness.
7. Some people claim to have seen Nessie and even photographed the monster.
8. Indeed, cameras have detected a large, moving object in the waters of the loch.
9. The mysterious serpent has inspired writers, scientists, and preservationists.
10. There may actually be some unknown creature living in this body of fresh water!

B. Identifying Common, Proper, Concrete, and Abstract Nouns

Which word in parentheses describes the boldfaced noun? Underline the correct one.

1. The very idea of monsters can inspire **fear** in children. (concrete, abstract)
2. A werewolf is a **human** who can turn into a wolf. (common, proper)
3. Werewolves have been part of mythology since the ancient **Sumerians** and Romans. (common, proper)
4. Contemporary folktales from **Germany** have added a modern twist to the lore of the werewolf. (common, proper)
5. Perhaps the **savagery** of real wolves inspired storytellers to create the myth of the werewolf. (concrete, abstract)
6. According to some tales, humans change themselves into werewolves by drinking water from a werewolf's **footprint**. (concrete, abstract)

Lesson 1

Nouns

More Practice

A. Finding Nouns

Underline the noun or nouns described in parentheses after each sentence.

1. The Black Death of medieval times created a time of fear and superstition. (proper noun)

2. According to legend, humans changed into werewolves when they put on wolfskins. (common noun)

3. Storytellers' tales of werewolves chilled their nervous listeners. (possessive noun)

4. Some stories tell of witches who could become wolves. (plural noun)

5. Saying the werewolf's name aloud would make it human again. (possessive noun)

6. A silver bullet should be used to kill a werewolf. (concrete noun)

7. In old stories, after the gunpowder cleared, the monsters were burned. (compound noun)

8. The full moon is linked to the appearance of werewolves. (singular noun)

9. Just imagine an entire pack of werewolves! (collective noun)

10. Stories of monsters have always created suspense. (abstract noun)

B. Using Nouns

Replace each boldfaced noun in the list with the type of noun specified in parentheses. The new noun should reflect the same idea or subject as the boldfaced noun.

EXAMPLES **author** (proper)   *Nathaniel Hawthorne*
fruit (compound)   *blueberry*

1. **occupation** (common) _____

2. **animal group** (collective) _____

3. **athlete** (proper) _____

4. **feeling** (abstract) _____

5. **tool** (concrete) _____

6. **fruit** (compound) _____

7. **governmental organization** (collective) _____

8. **reading material** (common) _____

9. **type of government** (abstract) _____

10. **weather phenomenon** (compound) _____

For use with Pupil's Edition pp. 6–8

Name _____ Date _____

Lesson 1

Nouns   *Application*

A. Using Nouns

Complete the paragraph by supplying nouns as indicated in parentheses. Write each word you would use on the blank line.

For sheer **(1. abstract noun)** nothing can beat a story about a sea monster. According to legend, sea monsters can be found in all bodies of water, especially the **(2. proper noun)**. The whale's size, the **(3. possessive noun)** teeth, and the squid's shape were combined to create legendary sea serpents. Despite their huge size, sea creatures are said to move with **(4. abstract noun)**. Even so, a **(5. collective noun)** of ships could be destroyed by the movements of a few whales. Early sailors thought the sounds of the dolphin were voices of lost **(6. plural noun)**. Their **(7. concrete noun)** sounded sad and lonely.

1. _____   5. _____

2. _____   6. _____

3. _____   7. _____

4. _____

B. Writing with Different Kinds of Nouns

Rewrite each of the following sentences, replacing each boldfaced noun with the kind of noun indicated in parentheses. You may need to add, subtract, or change the articles (*a, an, the*) in some sentences.

1. On safari, the photographers were hoping to spot an **elephant** (plural).

_____

2. For breakfast, Jamal likes **peaches** (compound).

_____

3. A good snorkeler has **fins** (abstract) and a **mask** (abstract).

_____

4. Only a **fraction** (compound) of our group went hiking in the **mountains** (proper).

_____

5. The snorkeler saw an **object** (concrete) near the **swimmer** (proper).

_____

6. Denise (common) admired the **beauty** (concrete) beneath the water's surface.

_____

7. The **person** (collective) won first place in the competition.

_____

8. Ms. Jackson (common) teaches canoeing skills every **weekend** (proper).

_____

Personal and Possessive Pronouns

Reteaching

A **pronoun** is a word used in place of a noun or another pronoun. The word that a pronoun stands for is called its **antecedent.**

> The <u>athlete</u> extended a hand to <u>his</u> opponent.
> ANTECEDENT   PRONOUN

Personal pronouns change form.

Personal Pronouns	Singular	Plural
First Person	I, me (my, mine)	we, us (our, ours)
Second Person	you (your, yours)	you (your, yours)
Third Person	he, him, she, her, it (his, her, hers, its)	they, them (their, theirs)

Possessive pronouns show ownership or relationship. The possessive pronouns are printed within parentheses in the chart above.

A. Finding Pronouns

Underline all the pronouns in the following sentences. Underline possessive pronouns twice.

> **EXAMPLE** Sometimes <u>I</u> think about <u>my</u> childhood.

1. In Hide-and-Seek, one player should cover her eyes.
2. The other players hide while she counts to 100, and then she shouts, "Ready or not, here I come!"
3. If she sees a player hiding, she must call his name, and if she beats him to home base, he is caught.
4. Players may race back to touch their home base before being found.
5. If they are successful, they can hide again in the next game.
6. You may have your own memories of playing a favorite childhood game.

B. Finding Pronouns and Antecedents

Underline all the pronouns in the following sentences. Underline their antecedents twice.

> **EXAMPLE** <u>Children</u> have played <u>their</u> games for generations.

1. Years ago children were asked to jump up and down on the earth so that its plants would be stimulated and grow taller.
2. Boys were probably the first rope jumpers, impressing girls with their speed.
3. Jump rope probably became more popular with girls when one girl added her songs and rhymes to the game.
4. In hopscotch, children hop over lines and test their balance.
5. Playing hopscotch as youngsters may have helped us learn our numbers.
6. Gail remembers, "One of my favorite games was tag."
7. If players didn't "freeze" when tagged, their movements could cost them the game.
8. Running was its own reward and being chased was exciting.

  For use with Pupil's Edition pp. 9–10

Name _____   Date _____

Personal and Possessive Pronouns   *More Practice*

A. Finding Pronouns and Antecedents

Underline each personal or possessive pronoun once and its antecedent twice.

EXAMPLE The <u>player</u> tipped <u>his</u> cap while walking toward the dugout.

1. The Mayor reviewed the budget and asked questions about it.
2. The discussion lasted for hours; it ended with an agreement.
3. Champollion used his knowledge of Greek and Coptic to understand the hieroglyphics on Rosetta Stone.
4. Billie Holiday was a jazz singer admired for the unique quality of her voice.
5. Susan, a junior in high school, has begun to think about her career goals.
6. Because it is understood by people of all nations, music is considered a universal language.
7. Its location near the Sahara Desert and the Niger River made Timbuktu a thriving commercial city.
8. Malcolm and Greg do their homework in the library.
9. Many Europeans use bicycles as a means of transportation to and from their work.
10. Ancient Ethiopian soldiers wore horses' skulls on their heads as helmets.

B. Using Pronouns

Complete each sentence with the appropriate personal pronoun. Write it on the line.

EXAMPLE Jackson hopes that _____*he*_____ will be elected team captain.

1. David arrived at softball tryouts and waited for _____ turn to bat.

2. Although _____ was nervous, Colin hit a double his first time at bat.

3. The parents sat in the bleachers but _____ cheers could be heard on the field.

4. The concession stand was open before the game, but _____ closed during the ninth inning.

5. The umpire was quite emphatic when _____ called strikes.

6. We are proud that _____ team will compete in the playoffs.

7. The players have practiced many hours for _____ big day.

8. While _____ were expected to win easily, they were surprised to find themselves in a real battle during the final game.

9. At the end of the ninth inning, we were upset to see _____ lead cut to only one run.

10. I could hardly believe _____ eyes when Jake hit a grand slam home run to win the game!

Lesson 2

Personal and Possessive Pronouns

Application

A. Writing Sentences with Pronouns

Write sentences using the types of pronouns indicated. Underline the required pronouns in your sentences.

1. personal pronoun in the first person plural

_____

2. possessive pronoun in the first person singular

_____

3. possessive pronoun in the second person plural

_____

4. personal pronoun in the third person singular

_____

5. possessive pronoun in the third person plural

_____

B. Writing with Pronouns

Write a short story about a pastime you enjoyed as a child. Use a variety of personal pronouns. After you are finished writing, circle each pronoun and draw an arrow leading from it to its antecedent.

_____

_____

_____

_____

_____

_____

_____

_____

_____

_____

_____

_____

For use with Pupil's Edition pp. 9–10

Lesson 3

Other Kinds of Pronouns

Reteaching

Some kinds of pronouns perform special functions in sentences.

CHAPTER 1

Type of pronoun	Function	Example
reflexive	reflects action back upon the subject of its sentence or clause	myself
intensive	emphasizes a noun or pronoun in the same sentence	herself
demonstrative	points out specific persons, places, things, or ideas	that, those
indefinite	refers to unidentified persons, places, things, or ideas	each, most
interrogative	introduces a question	who, what
relative	introduces a subordinate clause	who, that

Finding Pronouns

Underline all the pronouns in the following sentences.

1. While walking through the zoo's rain forest, I myself saw the anaconda slither under a shrub.

2. The gibbons amused themselves by swinging from tree to tree.

3. This is the largest bison in our zoo.

4. Many of the visitors were awed by the new aquarium.

5. Who is going to view the snake display?

6. Peacock feathers themselves are things of beauty.

7. Luckily, the animals seem undisturbed by the large number of people who come to see them.

8. Reuben looked for the aardvarks, but there were none.

9. Which is larger, the gorilla or the orangutan?

10. The curator, who oversees the animals, is usually a highly-trained zoologist.

11. Everyone entering the insect display was given a magnifying glass.

12. Melissa startled herself when she suddenly came upon the Komodo dragon.

13. Several of the zebras were thundering across the savanna area.

14. The veterinarian herself is responsible for the medical needs of the animals.

15. Animals that roam the grasslands include giraffes, zebras, and lions.

16. Is this a bighorn sheep or an ibex?

17. A trained zookeeper himself is directly responsible for the animals under his care.

18. What are the jaguars eating?

19. A colorful macaw was grooming itself high atop the palm tree.

20. The tracks of the ocelot differ from those of the lynx.

21. Whose was the idea of making zoos more naturalistic?

22. The platypus, whose appearance is quite unusual, is a native of Australia.

23. Often we can see ourselves reflected in the antics of the monkeys.

24. One of the pandas was eating a bamboo shoot.

25. Bactrian camels are over there; these are the Dromedaries.

26. The magnificent lion carried himself with grace and dignity.

Name _____ Date _____

Lesson 3 # Other Kinds of Pronouns

More Practice

A. Identifying Kinds of Pronouns

Identify the boldfaced pronoun in each of the following sentences by writing **reflexive, intensive, demonstrative, indefinite, interrogative,** or **relative** on the line.

1. **Which** is the oldest zoo, the Philadelphia Zoo or Central Park Zoo in New York? _____

2. Kodiak bears sunned **themselves** on the towering rocks. _____

3. **Those** are grizzlies, an especially vicious type of bear. _____

4. Karl Hagenbeck, **who** was a German animal dealer, developed the idea of placing zoo animals behind moats. _____

5. About 200 years ago, **anyone** with money could establish a small zoo. _____

6. You **yourself** could ride on the back of a giant tortoise. _____

7. **Few** of the earliest zoos made the preservation of animal species a priority. _____

8. The Arizona-Sonora Desert Museum, **which** is a small zoo in Tucson, contains native plants and animals. _____

9. Where are the wallabies **that** look so much like kangaroos? _____

10. The watchful mother quail guarded the babies **herself.** _____

B. Using Pronouns

Complete each sentence with the type of pronoun specified in parentheses. Write the pronoun on the line.

EXAMPLE When the foul ball dropped into the stands, (indefinite)

_____ *many* _____ of the fans tried to catch it.

1. Gloria found (reflexive) _____ dreading the visit to the dentist.

2. (indefinite) _____ in the school band practiced daily for the spring concert.

3. The doughnuts baked today are fresher than (demonstrative)

_____ made yesterday.

4. Rodney, (relative) _____ is running for class president, plastered posters all over school.

5. To (interrogative) _____ does the red convertible belong?

For use with Pupil's Edition pp. 11–13

Other Kinds of Pronouns

Application

A. Writing with Pronouns

Write six sentences about zoos and the animals you might see there. In each sentence, use the type of pronoun indicated in parentheses. Underline the required pronoun in each sentence.

1. (indefinite pronoun) _____

_____

2. (demonstrative pronoun)_____

_____

3. (interrogative pronoun) _____

_____

4. (reflexive pronoun) _____

_____

5. (relative pronoun) _____

_____

6. (intensive pronoun) _____

_____

B. Proofreading and Revising

Decide which pronouns have been used incorrectly in the paragraph below. Then rewrite the paragraph correctly on a different sheet of paper.

As you cautiously wind your way on the narrow path through thick vines, you suddenly find oneself face to face with a python dozing in a hollow log. You are not in the Amazon jungle; that is the rain forest exhibit at a modern zoo. Zoos itself have changed dramatically since they were first established in ancient times. Once mainly a display who showcased a ruler's wealth and power, zoos have become more animal centered and people friendly. Veterinarians whom specialize in the care of wild animals have become an integral part of zoo staffs. Trained zoologists that study diseases and habitats have improved the quality of life for both of the animals. As animals face extinction in the wild, the zoo has become a place who successfully breeds threatened species. Whom can predict what new ideas and technologies are in store for zoos in the future?

Verbs

Reteaching

A **verb** is a word used to express action, condition, or a state of being.

An **action verb** expresses a physical or mental action. An action verb that appears with a direct object (a person or thing that receives the action of the verb) is called a **transitive verb**. An action verb without a direct object is an **intransitive verb**.

A **linking verb** links the subject of a sentence to a word in the predicate. Some linking verbs are forms of *to be*, such as *am, is, was,* and *were*. Others, such as *appear, become, feel, look, remain, sound,* and *taste*, may express conditions. Some verbs such as *grow, feel,* and *taste* can be either action or linking verbs.

Auxiliary verbs, also called **helping verbs,** are combined with verbs to form **verb phrases.** Some common auxiliary verbs are forms of *be,* and *had, do, might, would, will, must, could,* and *would.*

A. Identifying Verbs

Underline the verb or verb phrase in each sentence. In the space above each verb, write **A** if it is an action verb, **L** if it is a linking verb, or **AUX** if it is an auxiliary verb.

1. Bonnie and Clyde were famous bank robbers during the 1930s.

2. In only two years, they killed a dozen innocent people.

3. They were wanted by the law for a variety of crimes.

4. Crime seemed romantic to Bonnie for about a year.

5. She and Clyde were traveling all over Texas together.

6. However, the life of a criminal is often harsh and short.

7. Bonnie was seriously injured in an auto accident at one point.

8. Clyde treated her at home without the help of doctors or hospitals.

9. Just before her death, Bonnie looked sick and old.

10. Bonnie and Clyde died in a hail of bullets during a police ambush in 1934.

B. Identifying Transitive and Intransitive Verbs

Underline the verb or verb phrase in each sentence. If the verb has a direct object, underline it twice. On the line, write **T** for a transitive verb and **I** for an intransitive verb.

1. Modern banks use the latest technology for surveillance of their offices. _____

2. Hidden cameras can videotape robbers without their knowledge. _____

3. Silent alarms notify police of a robbery attempt immediately. _____

4. Armed guards sometimes stand at the doors to the bank. _____

5. Convicted criminals pay for their crimes with years behind bars. _____

For use with Pupil's Edition pp. 14–16

Lesson 4

Verbs

More Practice

A. Identifying Verbs

Underline each verb once. If the verb has a direct object, underline the direct object twice. On the line, write **T** for transitive and **I** for intransitive.

1. The network canceled the show. _____

2. The pomegranate originated in Persia or Afghanistan. _____

3. Dogs have keen senses of hearing and smell. _____

4. The Egyptians used a uniform system of measurement. _____

5. Luckily, hard ice forms quickly over northern lakes. _____

6. Bees make 80,000 trips for a single pound of honey. _____

7. Of course, Hollywood attracts job seekers by the thousands. _____

8. In the fall, salmon spawn in the Sacramento River of California. _____

9. The classical music was coming from the next room. _____

10. Put mustard on the hot dog, please. _____

B. Using Action and Linking Verbs

Complete each of the following sentences with an appropriate action or linking verb. Then, in the lines, identify each verb you have used by writing **A** for action or **L** for linking.

1. The robbers _____ the train just before the bridge. _____

2. They _____ both skilled and ruthless. _____

3. The robbers _____ this job for months before this date. _____

4. Special bags on the train _____ over seven million dollars! _____

5. The thieves _____ the last car of the train. _____

6. The engineer _____ frightened. _____

7. Quickly, the robbers _____ the money bags off the train. _____

8. They _____ the money and went their separate ways. _____

9. At their hideout, some of the robbers _____ nervous. _____

10. They _____ at the sight of a low-flying plane and abandoned the farm. _____

11. Most of them _____ long prison terms for the robbery. _____

12. Investigators never _____ the money. _____

Lesson 4

Verbs

Application

A. Writing with Transitive and Intransitive Verbs

Use a form of each of the verbs listed below in two sentences, first as an intransitive verb and then as a transitive verb. Remember that a transitive verb must have a direct object.

EXAMPLE   swim (intransitive) *What is swimming in this pond?*
            (transitive)   *I swim 20 laps every day.*

1. study: (intransitive) _____

         (transitive) _____

2. eat: (intransitive) _____

         (transitive) _____

3. sail: (intransitive) _____

         (transitive) _____

4. drive: (intransitive) _____

         (transitive) _____

5. play: (intransitive) _____

         (transitive) _____

B. Proofreading

The writer of this paragraph was careless and omitted many verbs. Proofread the paragraph. Wherever a verb is missing, insert this proofreading symbol ∧ and write an action verb, a linking verb, or an auxiliary verb above it.

EXAMPLE   A traitor ^*is* someone who betrays his or her country.

     The most famous traitor in American history Benedict Arnold. Arnold once

a trusted general in the American army. He his bravery in a number of

dangerous battles against the British. He even injured seriously in defense of

his country. At one point, however, he was passed over for a promotion to

major general and resentful. Later, he reprimanded by George Washington for

actions that his critics opposed. Angry and bitter, Arnold with British forces in

a plan to force the military base at West Point, New York, to surrender. The

plan was discovered, and Arnold to New York City where he joined the British

Army. Although he acres of land in Canada, he spent his last years in the

West Indies, despised by the citizens of his own country.

For use with Pupil's Edition pp. 14–16

Adjectives

Reteaching

Adjectives modify noun or pronouns. They limit the meaning of the words they modify. Adjectives tell *what kind, which one, how many,* or *how much.*

<u>blue</u> ocean   <u>those</u> swimmers   <u>many</u> waves   <u>less</u> sunscreen

Articles are the most common adjectives. **Indefinite articles** (*a* and *an*) refer to unspecified members of groups of people, places, things, or ideas. *The* is the **definite article** that refers to a specific person, place, thing, or idea.

Proper adjectives are formed from proper nouns. They are capitalized and often end in *-n, -an, -ian, -ese,* or *-ish.* Some examples are *American, Japanese,* and *Polish.*

Finding Adjectives

Underline each adjective once and the word it modifies twice. Do not underline the articles.

1. Everyone enjoys a relaxing day at the beach.
2. Listening to the regular sound of waves hitting the beach can soothe jangled nerves.
3. I can see about ten umbrellas from where I am standing.
4. Those umbrellas protect sensitive skin from harmful sunlight.
5. I usually sunbathe in a place with fewer people, away from the crowd.
6. There I share the beach with a more seagulls than people.
7. I have gone there for several years.
8. The hot sand burned my feet.
9. When I go to that beach, I take cold drinks and salty snacks.
10. If I am lucky, I can read an interesting book for a few hours.
11. Little children play quietly near their parents.
12. I like to go for long walks on the beach.
13. I look for colorful shells and more rocks for my collection.
14. In the distance, I can see cruise ships on the way to Mexican resorts.
15. I imagine exciting trips to South American ports.
16. In my mind, I see Spanish galleons at the bottom of the ocean.
17. Chests with rare coins and gold necklaces lie a thousand feet below the surface.
18. The sight of a beach ball ends this daydream.
19. I returned to my soft blanket on the beach.
20. The angry gulls flew away when I disturbed them.
21. Soon they settle down, and a peaceful feeling descends on all of us.
22. Someday I would like to buy a house near the blue ocean.
23. I would sit on a comfortable chair on my porch and look at the sea.
24. I would watch gentle sunrises and spectacular sunsets every day.
25. I would never leave that beach again.

Adjectives

Lesson 5

More Practice

A. Identifying Adjectives

Underline each adjective once and the word it modifies twice. Some words are modified by more than one adjective. Do not underline articles. If the adjective is a proper adjective, write **P** above it.

1. Ted has taken several classes in photographic journalism.

2. The thoughtful audience remained silent throughout the performance.

3. The new models will use less fuel and get better mileage.

4. Gloria bought a yellow shirt and white jeans.

5. The senior class is studying European history.

6. Mauna Loa is a large volcano on one of the Hawaiian islands.

7. McIntosh apples usually are crisp and juicy.

8. The reporters asked insightful questions during the interview.

9. The agents found the secret documents in an old suitcase.

10. The miners talked to the press after the terrifying ordeal.

11. The refreshing water cooled my hot feet.

12. The travel magazine included an article about Japanese gardens.

B. Using Adjectives

Fill in the blanks with one or more adjectives to improve the descriptions of people who are enjoying a day at the beach. (Change the article preceding your adjectives from *a* to *an* if you use an adjective that begins with a vowel.)

The beach is filled with people looking for fun. **(1)** A _____ boy with a plastic bucket is digging in the sand. **(2)** His sister, dressed in a _____ swimsuit is building a sand castle next to him. **(3)** Back on the beach blanket, their mother, a young woman with _____ hair keeps close watch on them. **(4)** She calls to them in a _____ voice and points to a _____ bird near them. **(5)** An older couple dressed in _____ shorts enjoy a _____ walk along the beach. **(6)** Farther up the beach, a _____ group of young people are playing volleyball, shouting to each other in _____ voices. **(7)** One of the players seems especially _____, laughing and encouraging the other players. **(8)** All in all, it is a _____ day at the beach.

For use with Pupil's Edition pp. 17–19

Adjectives

Application

A. Writing Sentences with Adjectives

Revise these plain sentences by adding at least one adjective to each. You may also add descriptive phrases and clauses if you wish. Write your new sentence on the line. Underline the adjectives you have added.

> **EXAMPLE** The truck rumbled down the street.
> *The garbage truck rumbled down the narrow city street.*

1. The flower wilted in the sunlight.

_____

2. The milk tasted bad after a day in the cooler.

_____

3. A child pulled a wagon across the field.

_____

4. A siren broke the stillness of the night.

_____

5. Bring a sweater on the hike.

_____

B. Revising with Adjectives

On the lines below, write a paragraph about a day at the beach. Use at least ten adjectives in your paragraph. Include at least one proper adjective.

_____

_____

_____

_____

_____

_____

_____

_____

_____

_____

Lesson 6

Adverbs

Reteaching

Adverbs modify verbs, adjectives, or other adverbs. They answer the questions *where, when, how,* and *to what extent*. Adverbs are often formed by adding *–ly* to an adjective.

    go <u>there</u>   left <u>late</u>   speak <u>softly</u>   <u>nearly</u> complete

An **intensifier** is an adverb that defines the degree of an adjective or another adverb. Intensifiers always precede the adjectives or adverbs they modify.

    <u>really</u> easy   <u>too</u> tightly

Finding Adverbs

Underline all the adverbs in the following sentences.

1. One is never too old for a day at the zoo.
2. You must breathe more deeply at this altitude.
3. My ears and nose became quite cold as we waited for the bus.
4. As the balloon soared higher, we gripped the supports tightly with our hands.
5. Brad began to draft his report on T. S. Eliot immediately after supper.
6. The dispatcher gave directions clearly but swiftly to the rescue squad.
7. Patiently, Adam shelled the peas.
8. The tree trunks still smoldered long after the forest fire.
9. The ship sailed smoothly into the harbor.
10. Fun, food, and football go together.
11. The president vetoed the tax bill recently.
12. Emergency doctors quickly surrounded the incoming patient.
13. We sometimes wait for 20 minutes for this bus.
14. Drive straight down this road for a mile, and then turn right at the light.
15. The children tried hard to please their mother on her birthday.
16. My neighbor absolutely adores her cats.
17. Put the new bookcase there, please.
18. It rained heavily for most of the night.
19. This author writes exceptionally gripping novels.
20. He is surprisingly graceful for a heavy man.
21. Tomorrow the painters begin work on our house.
22. On a really quiet night, you can hear a train whistle far in the distance.
23. I still miss the friends that I left behind at my old school.
24. Many doctors say that bungee jumping is an unnecessarily dangerous sport.
25. Can you believe that the plane actually arrived early?

Adverbs

More Practice

A. Identifying Adverbs

Underline each adverb once and the word or words it modifies twice in each of the following sentences.

1. We cleaned the house thoroughly last week.
2. Sandra rearranged the furniture yesterday.
3. Drivers on the expressway must be very careful.
4. The votes for mayor are still being counted.
5. Jill does exceptionally fine work.
6. The Indian rugs were incredibly expensive.
7. I heard your question clearly, but I don't know the answer.
8. The city often holds concerts in the park.
9. The current here is too dangerous for swimming.
10. The wind was bitterly cold during the month of December.

B. Identifying Words Modified by Adverbs

Decide whether each adverb printed in boldface type modifies a verb, an adjective, or another adverb. Write **V, ADJ,** or **ADV** on the line.

1. The dictator **callously** disregarded the wishes of his people. _____

2. The stadium was **virtually** silent after our heartbreaking loss. _____

3. My grandparents **usually** go to bed at ten o'clock. _____

4. We were **very** definitely told to come to this door. _____

5. The sun **never** shines brightly in this corner of my garden. _____

6. The sound of your voice is **barely** audible in this loud room. _____

7. This speaker chooses her words **quite** carefully. _____

8. **First,** slowly open the window. _____

9. You need to be **more** meticulous when you do your proofreading. _____

10. We were **extremely** shocked when we heard the bad news yesterday. _____

11. The library closes **early** on Saturdays during the summer. _____

12. Have you learned **yet** who won the championship? _____

13. The speaker was **somewhat** annoyed that the microphone wasn't
    working properly. _____

14. The rock band arrived at the concert **late** and went right on stage. _____

15. The wind blew **surprisingly** strongly all night. _____

Lesson 6

Adverbs

Application

A. Writing Sentences with Adverbs

Revise each of these sentences by adding at least one adverb. You may also add
descriptive phrases and clauses if you wish. Write your new sentence on the line.
Underline the adverbs you have added.

> **EXAMPLE** The fly buzzed.
> *The fly buzzed <u>annoyingly</u> in my ear.*

1. The politicians debated the issue.

_____

2. The lead guitar player sang the slow songs.

_____

3. The snow fell.

_____

4. The teacher moved around the room.

_____

5. I pass this house on my way to school.

_____

B. Writing with Adverbs

This paragraph is a review of a pilot for a television series. The review could be
improved by the addition of adverbs. On the lines below, rewrite each numbered
sentence. Include an adverb that modifies the boldfaced verb.

> **(1)** I **switched** my television on with hope in my heart. I had heard
> good things about this possible series. **(2)** For one thing, the producers
> **had assembled** a great cast. **(3)** All the actors were well respected and
> **experienced. (4)** The writers **had** good credentials, having worked on the hit
> series *In My Opinion.* **(5)** But after a few minutes, I **felt** disappointed. Where
> were the clever lines? Where was the chemistry between these actors?
> **(6)** The actors **spoke** their lines. **(7)** They **seemed** detached from the story, and
> I understand why. My advice to them would be to disconnect themselves
> from this certain flop as quickly as possible and concentrate on more
> promising ventures.

_____

_____

_____

_____

_____

For use with Pupil's Edition pp. 20–22

Prepositions

Reteaching

A **preposition** shows the relationship between a noun or pronoun and another word in the sentence. Some common prepositions include the following: *about, before, by, during, on,* and *under.* Prepositions formed from more than one word are **compound prepositions.** Some examples of compound prepositions are *according to, in place of, because of,* and *instead of.*

A **prepositional phrase** consists of a preposition, its object, and any modifiers of the object. The **object of the preposition** is the noun or a pronoun that follows the preposition.

> Hang the antique quilt **with** blue <u>patches</u> **on** the <u>wall</u>. (*With* and *on* are prepositions. *Patches* and *wall* are the objects of the prepositions.)

A. Finding Prepositions

Underline the preposition in each sentence. Remember that compound prepositions have two or more words.

1. A quilt is simply a cover for a bed.
2. But, to many women, it has a deeper significance.
3. In colonial America, women often sewed and assembled quilts together.
4. These quilting parties were a chance for much-needed socialization.
5. Quilts were pieced together from extra cloth swatches.
6. Each piece reminded the quilter of a loved one.
7. Quilts were often presented as gifts.
8. Instead of money, young newlyweds would receive a quilt.
9. Today, quilts have regained much of the popularity they had years ago.
10. By means of quilts, people today can touch the past.

B. Identifying Prepositional Phrases

Underline the prepositional phrases in the following sentences.

1. Armadillos rarely give birth to quadruplets.
2. Between the two houses is a large white fence.
3. Our class met some visitors from China.
4. Their charming cottage is near Lake Cumberland.
5. Have you eaten anything since breakfast?
6. The baseball game was canceled on account of rain.
7. We looked inside the submarine.
8. Everyone except Jan was there.
9. Hernando always plays according to the rules.
10. The seahorse carries its eggs in a pouch.

Name _____   Date _____

Lesson 7

Prepositions

More Practice

A. Identifying Prepositional Phrases

Underline each prepositional phrase once. Underline the object of the preposition twice. A sentence may have more than one prepositional phrase.

1. Woodworking means forming wood into useful or beautiful objects.
2. A competent woodworker needs a number of tools for the job.
3. For measuring, you need rulers and framing squares.
4. A woodworker cannot function without decent cutting tools.
5. One familiar tool for cutting is the handsaw.
6. According to most modern woodworkers, however, an electric saw is the preferred tool.
7. With a plane, the woodworker shapes and smoothes the wood in fine items.
8. Drills help woodworkers make holes so they can connect pieces of wood with screws.
9. Rubbing with abrasive sandpaper makes surfaces smooth enough for the last step in the process.
10. Woodworkers use simple paintbrushes for the final touch—staining or painting the wood.

B. Writing with Prepositional Phrases

Add a prepositional phrase to each sentence using the preposition specified in parentheses. Write your new sentence on the line.

EXAMPLE There is a cabin. (in)
There is a cabin in the woods.

1. We set up camp. (after)

   _____

2. Flowers grew. (near)

   _____

3. I would like fresh tomatoes. (instead of)

   _____

4. The hikers took flashlights. (in addition to)

   _____

5. I always run. (past)

   _____

6. We took the ferry. (across)

   _____

7. Everyone liked the pizza. (except)

   _____

For use with Pupil's Edition pp. 23–25

CHAPTER 1

Lesson 7

Prepositions

Application

A. Writing with Prepositional Phrases

Replace the prepositional phrase in each sentence. Write your new sentence on the line. Use a different preposition and a new object of the preposition.

> EXAMPLE   The squirrel ran **up the tree.**
> *The squirrel ran into the street.*

1. **Despite my tiredness,** I had a great time.

_____

2. The rabbit hid **underneath the tall bush.**

_____

3. The batter hit the ball **toward first base.**

_____

4. I dropped my keys **behind the sofa cushions.**

_____

5. A strange apparition floated **between me and the door.**

_____

6. The river flowed **over its banks.**

_____

B. Writing with Prepositional Phrases

Use all of these prepositional phrases in an original story. Write your story on the lines below.

beyond that hill	according to legend	against all expectations
down the road	above the noise	inside my head
after sunrise	because of my curiosity	past a misshapen tree

_____

_____

_____

_____

_____

_____

_____

_____

_____

Conjunctions and Interjections

Reteaching

A **conjunction** connects words or groups of words. A **coordinating conjunction** connects words or word groups that have equal importance in a sentence. The following are coordinating conjunctions: *and, but, for, nor, or, so,* and *yet.*

Correlative conjunctions are pairs of conjunctions that join words or groups of words. Some correlative conjunctions are *both . . . and, either . . . or,* and *not only . . . but also.*

Subordinating conjunctions introduce subordinate clauses—clauses that cannot stand alone as complete sentences—and join them to independent clauses. The following are some examples subordinating conjunctions: *after, although, as, because, if, since, so that, until, when,* and *while.*

A **conjunctive adverb** is used to express relationships between independent clauses. Some common conjunctive adverbs are *also, consequently, however, nevertheless, still, therefore, besides,* and *otherwise.*

An **interjection** is a word or phrase that expresses an emotion or strong feeling. A strong interjection is followed by an exclamation point. A mild interjection is followed by a comma. Some examples of interjections are *oh, well,* and *yippee.*

Identifying Conjunctions and Interjections

Underline the conjunctions and the conjunctive adverbs in the following sentences. Draw parentheses around any interjections. Remember that correlative conjunctions are word pairs, so underline both parts.

1. Exercise is a great way to build endurance and increase your energy level.
2. Not only is exercise good for you but it also is fun.
3. Although setting up an exercise schedule takes time, it is well worth the effort.
4. Many teenagers take up running, but their interest in that sport may fade.
5. As people age, they exercise less and less.
6. At least 30 minutes of exercise three times a week is recommended; however, not enough people follow those guidelines.
7. It takes discipline to exercise every day; besides, no one seems to have time for it.
8. "Oh, I'll get to that some other day," people tell themselves.
9. Few activities are so important yet so easily ignored.
10. Decide today to begin an exercise regimen, and don't let yourself off so easily.
11. You may choose to take up either racquetball or running if you like strenuous exercise.
12. You might not have access to state-of-the-art facilities; still, you can be sure that there is a sport that is right for you.
13. You will say, "Wow! I wish I had started this before!" when you see the difference exercise makes in your energy level.
14. Whether you are a confirmed couch potato or a reasonably active person, exercise can develop your endurance, strength, and flexibility.
15. Be sure to begin today; otherwise, you may put it off forever.

For use with Pupil's Edition pp. 26–29

Lessons 8–9

Conjunctions and Interjections

More Practice

A. Identifying Conjunctions and Interjections

Underline the conjunctions and conjunctive adverbs in the following sentences.
Draw parentheses around any interjections.

1. Nutrition is the science that focuses on what we eat and how our bodies use that fuel.

2. Well, whether we like this fact or not, the foods we eat make a difference in our health.

3. Although we may enjoy greasy foods, they are not particularly good for us.

4. We must pay attention to our body's needs; otherwise, we may face health problems down the road.

5. Your body tries hard to cope when you supply it with only junk food.

6. Because you are young, you think your good health will last forever.

7. The best way to maintain your health is through sensible eating habits; consequently, you should eat a balanced diet.

8. Yes, a balanced diet includes breads, meat, milk products, fruits, and vegetables.

9. Unless you take in enough minerals, your growth may be affected adversely.

10. Both meat and whole-grain cereals provide you with vitamins.

B. Writing with Conjunctions, Conjunctive Adverbs, and Interjections

Complete the following sentences with a conjunction, a conjunctive adverb, or an interjection.

EXAMPLE My goal is to run a marathon, _____*but*_____ I haven't tried one yet.

1. _____ the downpour began, the umpire stopped the game.

2. I will be out of town this weekend; _____, I can't come to your party.

3. Brad worked on his science project for weeks, _____ he hopes to win a superior rating.

4. _____ the president _____ the vice president will attend the funeral.

5. _____! My foot fell asleep!

6. _____ we go to the beach _____ we go to the mountains, we'll have a great vacation.

7. It is raining today; _____, we'll have to postpone the picnic.

8. _____! I got an A on the test!

9. Play will resume _____ the groundskeepers remove the tarpaulin.

CHAPTER 1

Conjunctions and Interjections

Application

A. Proofreading

Proofread the following paragraph. When you find a place where conjunctions, conjunctive adverbs, or interjections would improve the paragraph, insert this proofreading symbol ∧ and write your additions above it. Be sure to add at least one interjection.

Today I had to give a speech in English class. The assignment had two parts: to explain a process to prepare some visual aids. I thought I knew my material, I'm not sure I did very well at first. Both my teacher my classmates looked kind of confused while I spoke. Finally, I began to concentrate on what I was saying, the situation improved. I even coaxed a few laughs from my audience. Not only did I start to make sense, I began to have fun. I gave this speech, I have learned something about myself. I will never be a great public speaker, I will not fear public speaking either.

B. Writing an Explanation Using Conjunctions and Interjections

Suppose you are abducted by kindly aliens. After they take you aboard their ship, they ask you to explain your eating requirement needs so they can care for you properly. Write a paragraph to give them. Use at least two coordinating conjunctions, two subordinating conjunctions, one correlative conjunction, one conjunctive adverb, and two interjections. Write each of the conjunctions and interjections under the appropriate heading below your paragraph.

_____

_____

_____

_____

_____

Coordinating Conjunctions   **Subordinating Conjunctions**

_____   _____

_____   _____

Correlative Conjunction   **Conjunctive Adverb**

_____   _____

Interjections

_____

_____

For use with Pupil's Edition pp. 26–29

Simple Subjects and Predicates

Reteaching

Every sentence needs both a subject and a predicate. The **subject** tells whom or what the sentence is about. The **predicate** tells what the subject is or does or what happens to the subject. The **simple subject** is the key word or words in the complete subject. The **simple predicate** is the verb or verb phrase that tells something about the subject.

Daily <u>life</u> in the American colonies <u>comes</u> alive in restored Williamsburg.
SIMPLE SUBJECT   SIMPLE PREDICATE

<u>Vacationers</u> <u>should consider</u> a visit to this fascinating site.
SIMPLE SUBJECT SIMPLE PREDICATE

Identifying Simple Subjects and Simple Predicates

Underline the simple subject once and the simple predicate twice.

EXAMPLE The historic <u>city</u> of Williamsburg <u>attracts</u> thousands of tourists.

1. Williamsburg is a restored colonial town in Virginia.
2. At this tourist attraction, costumed guides show visitors around their town.
3. In the springtime, gardens are filled with daffodils and tulips.
4. Hungry tourists enjoy dinners in candle-lit taverns and restaurants.
5. Uniformed soldiers perform maneuvers on the commons to the delight of both children and adults.
6. At some sites, skilled craftspersons practice long-forgotten arts such as blacksmithing and candlemaking.
7. Williamsburg served as the capital of the Virginia Colony from 1699 to 1779.
8. In 1765, Patrick Henry delivered his famous speech in the Williamsburg Capitol.
9. English colonists chose the site for its good soil drainage and pleasant climate
10. At first, residents called the colony Middle Plantation.
11. Later, colonists renamed the town Williamsburg in honor of King William III.
12. During *publick times,* fancy balls were held in the bustling town.
13. Williamsburg was the site of the first newspaper in Virginia, *The Virginia Gazette.*
14. John D. Rockefeller, Jr., supported the town's restoration during the 1920s.
15. A historic plantation is located just outside Williamsburg.
16. Inside the homes of Williamsburg, rooms are decorated in the colonial style.
17. Even the streets are brick and cobblestone instead of modern asphalt.
18. In April, flowering trees fill the air with a sweet smell.
19. Pink and white blossoms make the little town colorful and inviting.
20. A Williamsburg visit will be an enjoyable step back into time.

Simple Subjects and Predicates

More Practice

A. Identifying Simple Subjects and Simple Predicates

Underline the simple subject once and the simple predicate twice in each of the following sentences.

EXAMPLE The <u>city</u> of Boston <u>hosts</u> an exciting sports event every spring.

1. The Boston Marathon is an annual 26-mile race.
2. Many runners come from all over the world for this event.
3. The race begins in a suburb of Boston.
4. The course takes runners around the Massachusetts countryside.
5. The night before the race, many runners eat pasta dinners.
6. These carbohydrates give the runners energy and stamina.
7. During the race, many runners hit "the wall" after 20 miles.
8. Some racers are stopped by this phenomenon.
9. Approximately 6,000 people enter the competition each year.
10. Despite the tension and exhaustion, many contestants return again and again.

B. Identifying Complete Sentences

Some of the following items are complete sentences and some are fragments. If the item is a complete sentence, write **CS** on the line. If the item is a fragment, write either **SS** or **SP** to identify whether the sentence is missing a simple subject or a simple predicate.

1. Our capital city, Washington, D.C., is a sightseer's paradise. _____

2. The imposing figure of Abraham Lincoln at the Lincoln Memorial. _____

3. Tourists the city at cherry blossom time each spring. _____

4. The White House stands on lush grounds in the downtown area. _____

5. May view world-famous works of art at the National Gallery of Art. _____

6. Travelers the efficient underground train system every day. _____

7. Conduct tours of the Capitol Building throughout the year. _____

8. The Washington Monument is the tallest structure in the city. _____

9. Is located between the White House and the Capitol. _____

10. The Smithsonian Institution several separate and fascinating museums. _____

For use with Pupil's Edition pp. 38–40

Simple Subjects and Predicates   *Application*

A. Writing Subjects and Predicates

Write sentences on the lines below by adding both a subject and a predicate to each fragment. Do not use the fragment as the subject of the sentence.

1. deep under the waters of the Atlantic _____

_____

2. in the window seat on the plane _____

_____

3. because of her allergies _____

_____

4. after spring training _____

_____

5. out of the alien ship _____

_____

6. beside a mountain stream _____

_____

B. Revising

Read this paragraph carefully. It contains several sentence fragments. When you find a sentence fragment, use this proofreading symbol ∧ to add a subject or a predicate.

is built
EXAMPLE   San Francisco∧on more than 40 hills.

One of the most popular tourist attractions on the West Coast San

Francisco, California. Is known for its breathtaking views of the San Francisco

Bay and the Pacific Ocean. The Golden Gate Bridge this lovely city with

suburbs to the north. Residents good at driving on steep inclines. In fact,

some of the steepest and most winding streets in the country in San

Francisco. No should leave without a look at the famous cable cars. The clang

of their bells in the streets of the city. Every tourist should also Fisherman's

Wharf for a taste of good, fresh seafood.

CHAPTER 2

Complete Subjects and Predicates

Reteaching

The **complete subject** includes the simple subject and all the words that modify it. The **complete predicate** includes the verb and all the words that modify it. Every word in a sentence is either part of the complete subject or part of the complete predicate.

The ticket booths at the ballpark opened at six o'clock.
COMPLETE SUBJECT   **COMPLETE PREDICATE**

A. Identifying Complete Subjects and Complete Predicates

Underline the complete subject once and the complete predicate twice.

EXAMPLE The winning team enthusiastically celebrated the victory.

1. All of the players took batting practice before the game.
2. Banks of bright lights shone on the field.
3. The grass of the baseball diamond glowed a brilliant green in the lights.
4. Helpful ushers showed fans to their seats.
5. The voice on the loudspeaker announced today's lineup.
6. The opposing pitcher was known for his speedy fast ball.
7. A confident manager waved to the crowd with his cap.
8. One of the league's most dangerous hitters stepped up to the plate.
9. A roar of support rose from the sold-out ballpark.
10. The crack of the bat was followed by the sound of fireworks.

B. Identifying Complete Subjects and Complete Predicates

Decide whether the underlined words in each sentence are the complete subject or the complete predicate. Write **Subject** or **Predicate** on the line.

1. The carousel had 20 colorful horses.   _____

2. Eric broke the school record for the high jump.   _____

3. An alert student noticed an unusual smell in the hall.   _____

4. The man with the mustache waited at the bus stop every day.   _____

5. An elderly couple lived in a cabin by a lake.   _____

6. Emily posted an e-mail message to her friend.   _____

7. The other team was late for the big game.   _____

8. The clear pictures from Mars delighted the scientists.   _____

9. The swimming instructor blew a loud whistle.   _____

10. The disc jockeys announced the winners on the air.   _____

For use with Pupil's Edition pp. 41–42

Complete Subjects and Predicates
More Practice

A. Identifying Complete Subjects and Predicates

Draw a vertical line between the complete subject and the complete predicate in each of the following sentences.

EXAMPLE The members of the marching band | took a bus to the game.

1. The crowd swayed with the rhythm of the cheerleaders' chant.
2. The football players seemed energized by the crowd's cheers.
3. The veteran quarterback looked for an opening in the other team's defense.
4. The running back avoided attackers on his way down the field.
5. The fans in the stands cheered after the touchdown.
6. The trombone section of the band started the wave.
7. The coach's assistant in the red jersey helped an injured player off the field.
8. A series of black clouds threw shadows onto the field.
9. A sudden downpour dampened some fans' enthusiasm for the game.
10. Hundreds of excited fans made their way to the exits.

B. Using Complete Subjects and Predicates

Decide whether the following groups of words could be used as a complete subject or a complete predicate. Write **CS** for a complete subject or **CP** for a complete predicate. Then, use each group of words to write a complete sentence, adding a complete subject or complete predicate as necessary.

EXAMPLE The sound of garbage trucks *woke the entire neighborhood.*   CS

1. The officer on duty _____. _____
2. _____ stopped in front of the library. _____
3. The tiny extraterrestrials _____. _____
4. _____ played the game of their lives. _____
5. _____ felt proud and relieved. _____
6. The last bus of the night _____. _____
7. _____ began after the concert. _____
8. The new aquarium _____. _____
9. _____ bought tickets to the movie. _____
10. The stairs to the loft _____. _____

Complete Subjects and Predicates

Application

A. Using Complete Subjects and Predicates

Choose from these subjects and predicates to complete the paragraph below.
Write the complete subjects and complete predicates on the lines. Remember
to use proper capitalization.

The game of tennis   was soon called *lawn tennis*
made some variations on the old game   has become popular around the world
the players   held the first tennis tournament ever
The tennis tournament

_____ began in France around 1100.

Then, _____ batted a ball back and forth across a net

with the palms of their hands. Modern tennis began much later.

In 1874, Major Walter Clopton Wingfield _____

_____ .

His new game _____ .

In 1877, the All England Croquet and Lawn Tennis Club _____

_____ . _____

_____ took place in Wimbledon,

outside of London. Since those early days, tennis _____

_____ .

B. Writing with Complete Subjects and Complete Predicates

Imagine that you have taken these notes for a report. As you review your notes,
you will rewrite fragments as complete sentences. Write the following notes as
sentences that have complete subjects and complete predicates. If you like, you
may combine two or more fragments in a single sentence.

Ice climbing—as a sport in the 1960s. Hike into mountains. Find frozen
waterfalls. Hundreds of feet high. Need special equipment. Two axes with
serrated teeth. Climbers have metal cleats on their boots. Push cleats into the
ice. Ropes with them on their climbs. For tying themselves to screws in the
ice. Dangerous sport. Only with other climbers.

_____

_____

_____

_____

_____

For use with Pupil's Edition pp. 42–43

Lesson 3

Compound Subjects and Verbs

Reteaching

A **compound subject** is made up of two or more subjects that share a verb. The subjects are joined by a conjunction, or connecting word, such as *and, or,* or *but.*

<u>Stocks</u> and <u>bonds</u> <u>are traded</u> in the stock market.
COMPOUND SUBJECT   SIMPLE VERB

A **compound verb** is made up of two or more verbs or verb phrases that are joined by a conjunction and have the same subject.

<u>Brokers</u> <u>buy</u> and <u>sell</u> stocks.
SIMPLE   COMPOUND
SUBJECT   VERB

A **compound predicate** is made up of a compound verb and all the words that go with each verb.

<u>Government officials</u> <u>oversee the workings of the stock market and verify its stability.</u>
SIMPLE SUBJECT   COMPOUND PREDICATE

Identifying Compound Subjects and Compound Verbs

Underline the compound subject or the compound verb in each sentence. Then, on the line, write **CS** for compound subject or **CV** for compound verb.

EXAMPLE Federal laws <u>regulate</u> and <u>oversee</u> the stock market. ___CV___

1. Companies and corporations sell shares to stockholders. _____

2. Stocks usually increase or decrease in value over time. _____

3. Profits and losses by a company affect its stock's value. _____

4. Good times and good management increase a stock's value. _____

5. Bad management hurts or sometimes destroys a company. _____

6. Stockbrokers check prices and make trades for buyers. _____

7. Millionaires and ordinary people trade stocks worth millions of dollars. _____

8. The NYSE and NASDAQ are two stock exchanges in the United States. _____

9. Prosperity and rising prices bring about a bull market. _____

10. Stockholders sometimes gain and sometimes lose money. _____

11. New York and Tokyo are sites of stock exchanges. _____

12. Today, people use the Internet and make trades on computers. _____

13. Someday, the shouting of brokers and the wild scenes on the floor of the stock market will be history. _____

14. Investors still want and need the help of stockbrokers now. _____

15. On any given day, the price of a stock rises or falls. _____

CHAPTER 2

Lesson 3

Compound Subjects and Verbs

More Practice

Writing Sentences with Compound Subjects and Compound Verbs

Rewrite each of the following sentences, making the part indicated in parentheses compound. Make sure the subjects and verbs agree in number.

EXAMPLE We love soccer. (subject)
Jess and I love soccer.

EXAMPLE The little girl skipped down the sidewalk. (verb)
The little girl skipped and ran down the sidewalk.

1. We returned the books to the library. (subject)

_____

2. The fireworks sparkled in the dark summer sky. (verb)

_____

3. After the meeting, the secretary will file a report. (verb)

_____

4. Ellen studied all day at the library. (subject)

_____

5. Tulips are welcome signs of spring. (subject)

_____

6. Last Saturday, Kevin washed the car. (verb)

_____

7. Two soups were listed on today's menu at the cafeteria. (subject)

_____

8. Experienced gardeners water their plants regularly. (verb)

_____

9. The talented star directed her latest movie. (verb)

_____

10. Boxes are stacked in the corner of Grandmother's attic. (subject)

_____

Compound Subjects and Verbs

Application

A. Sentence Combining with Compound Subjects and Compound Verbs

Combine each pair of sentences by using a compound subject or a compound verb. Be sure that the subject and the verb agree in number.

EXAMPLE Spices improve the taste of food. Herbs improve the taste of food.
Spices and herbs improve the taste of food.

1. Many paintings are on display at the art museum. Many sculptures are on display, too.

   _____

2. Melinda slipped on the ice. She tumbled down hard.

   _____

3. Steve has seen that movie. Daesonn has seen that movie.

   _____

4. The custodian enters each room at night. He turns off the lights.

   _____

5. The exercise leader lay on the mat. She exhaled completely.

   _____

B. More Sentence Combining

Revise the following paragraph, using compound subjects and compound verbs, to combine sentences with similar ideas. Write the new paragraph on the lines below.

   During the Great Depression, banks closed. Businesses closed. Stores closed. People lost their jobs. They became penniless. Many stocks became worthless. Bonds became worthless, too. Around the world, many countries were facing the same problems. England was affected by the Depression. Germany was affected by the Depression. In Germany, poverty created great misery. Poverty led to the rise of Adolf Hitler. The Great Depression lasted until countries began producing war materials for World War II. The widespread misery also lasted until that time.

   _____

   _____

   _____

   _____

   _____

Kinds of Sentences

Reteaching

A **declarative sentence** makes a statement and ends with a period.

> Maureen is an avid hiker.

An **interrogative sentence** asks a question and ends with a question mark.

> Has Maureen hiked to the lake before?

An **imperative sentence** gives a command and usually ends with a period. If the command is strong, it may end with an exclamation point.

> Come with me. Watch out for the snake!

An **exclamatory sentence** expresses strong emotions and ends with an exclamation point.

> How beautiful this view is!

Identifying Kinds of Sentences

Identify each sentence below as **DEC** for declarative, **INT** for interrogative, **IMP** for imperative, or **EXC** for exclamatory. Add the proper punctuation mark at the end of each sentence.

1. Where is the Baseball Hall of Fame   _____

2. In Greek mythology, Mercury was the messenger of the gods   _____

3. How exciting it is to watch trapeze artists   _____

4. Do you know what the Dewey Decimal System is   _____

5. That's incredible   _____

6. Look in the card catalog for a book on Amelia Earhart   _____

7. What country gave the Statue of Liberty to the United States   _____

8. In 1990, Dallas, Texas, ranked eighth among the U.S.'s largest cities   _____

9. Don't try to change my mind   _____

10. New England's Shaker communities cared for homeless children   _____

11. The Dutch artist Vincent van Gogh is famous for his bold use of color   _____

12. Have you ever been to the art museum   _____

13. What an exciting dancing style he has   _____

14. Wait at the corner for the bus downtown   _____

15. The book under my bed is overdue   _____

16. Did you forget your gloves   _____

17. How strange this fruit tastes   _____

For use with Pupil's Edition pp. 45–46

Name _____   Date _____

Lesson 4

Kinds of Sentences   *More Practice*

Using Different Kinds of Sentences

Add the correct end punctuation to each of these sentences. Then rewrite
the sentences, adding or changing words as needed, to satisfy the instructions
in parentheses.

> **EXAMPLE**   Artist Mary Cassatt spent many years in France
>   (Change to a question.)
>   *Where did Mary Cassatt live for many years?*

1. What an eye she had for light and color
(Change to a declarative sentence.)

_____

2. Her paintings often show ordinary people in their daily activities
(Change to an interrogative sentence.)

_____

3. Can you see the regard for the tasks of women in her work
(Change to an imperative sentence.)

_____

4. Mary Cassatt painted in the impressionist style for much of her career
(Change to an interrogative sentence.)

_____

5. Her images of women and children are loving and delicate
(Change to an exclamatory sentence.)

_____

6. Everyday situations took on importance and dignity in her paintings
(Change to an interrogative sentence.)

_____

7. Notice the difference between her earlier and her later works
(Change to a declarative sentence.)

_____

8. How beautiful her Japanese-inspired woodcuts are
(Change to a declarative sentence.)

_____

9. Cassatt was a good friend of impressionist painter Edgar Degas
(Change to an interrogative sentence.)

_____

10. Will you look for Mary Cassatt's work in your local museum
(Change to an imperative sentence.)

_____

CHAPTER 2

For use with Pupil's Edition pp. 45–46

GRAMMAR, USAGE, AND MECHANICS WORKBOOK   **35**

Kinds of Sentences

Application

A. Writing Different Kinds of Sentences in a Monologue

Imagine that you are a guide in an art museum. Your job is to show art students various paintings and sculptures. Write the speech that you might give. Use at least one of each of the following types of sentences: declarative, interrogative, imperative, and exclamatory. Use the correct punctuation at the end of each sentence. Remember to involve your students as much as possible in your lesson.

_____

_____

_____

_____

_____

_____

_____

_____

_____

B. Writing Different Kinds of Sentences in a Dialogue

Write a dialogue that two visitors to an art museum might have as they look at the paintings. Again, use at least one of each kind of sentence: declarative, interrogative, imperative, and exclamatory. Enclose each speaker's words in quotation marks. Use the correct punctuation at the end of each sentence, inside the quotation marks.

_____

_____

_____

_____

_____

_____

_____

_____

_____

For use with Pupil's Edition pp. 45–46

Lesson 5

Subjects in Unusual Positions

Reteaching

In an **inverted sentence,** the subject comes after the verb or part of the verb phrase.

> Into the room <u>walked</u> <u>Tony</u>.
>   VERB   SUBJECT

Sometimes the words *here* or *there* come before the subject or the verb.

> Here <u>are</u> the <u>books</u> from the list.
>   VERB   SUBJECT

In a **question,** the subject usually comes after the verb or inside the verb phrase.

> <u>Is</u> your <u>phone</u> <u>working</u> properly?
> VERB   SUBJECT

In an **imperative sentence,** the subject is usually *you*. Often, *you* is not stated; it is understood.

> <u>Read</u> the label on your medicine bottle carefully.
> VERB   (UNDERSTOOD SUBJECT IS YOU.)

Finding Subjects and Verbs in Unusual Positions

In the following sentences, underline the simple subject once and the verb or verb phrase twice. If the subject is understood, write **You** in parentheses on the line.

1. Write home as soon as possible. _____

2. There is an exhibit of Ray's photographs at the bank. _____

3. Does Francine play tennis on the school team? _____

4. Always check your answers on a test. _____

5. Here are the tickets to the concert. _____

6. How much money did the group raise for charity? _____

7. On the front door hung a large wreath. _____

8. There will be a meeting of the French Club on Thursday. _____

9. In Lancaster County, Pennsylvania, are many Amish families. _____

10. Here is the key to the mailbox. _____

11. Into the rain forest went the photographers. _____

12. Save me a place in line. _____

13. There was too much noise backstage. _____

14. Has Quintero heard this new CD? _____

15. What did Anna tell you? _____

16. To your left is the mansion of the governor. _____

Lesson 5

Subjects in Unusual Positions

More Practice

A. Writing Sentences

In the following sentences, underline the simple subject once and the verb twice. Then rewrite each sentence so that the subject comes before the verb.

> **EXAMPLE** There <u>are</u> just a few important <u>rules</u> in this game.
> *A few rules are important in this game.*

1. There is a new drummer playing with this band.

   _____

2. Along the path grow colorful wildflowers.

   _____

3. Were you speaking to me?

   _____

4. Here are the latest research findings.

   _____

5. In the house across the street lives a family with eight children.

   _____

B. Writing Sentences

Rewrite these sentences, following the directions in parentheses. Underline the simple subject of your sentence once and the verb twice. If the subject is an understood *you*, write **you** in parentheses after your sentence.

> **EXAMPLE** The tables are there. (Begin with *There.*)
> *There <u>are</u> the <u>tables</u>.*

1. You must write your name at the top of the page. (Change this to an imperative sentence.)

   _____

2. Bill rode his bike to school. (Change the sentence to a question.)

   _____

3. A package for you is on the front steps. (Begin with *There.*)

   _____

4. Under the snow were found the remains of a mountain cabin. (Begin with the words *The remains.* Use a traditional word order.)

   _____

5. You must pay for your tickets at the booth. (Change this to an imperative sentence.)

   _____

For use with Pupil's Edition pp. 47–49

Subjects in Unusual Positions

Application

A. Revising Using a Variety of Sentence Orders

The writer of this paragraph decided never to use the traditional word order of subject before verb. In all of the paragraph's sentences, the subject is found in an unusual position. Rewrite the paragraph, this time using a variety of sentence orders to make the paragraph more understandable and pleasing to the reader.

> Across the frozen tundra race the contestants in the Iditarod. Pulled by dogs are the sleds. Why do the racers go on? In their hearts is a love for the frozen North and its traditions. There are many hardships on this grueling race. Along certain parts of the trail lurk special dangers. At some points, there are high winds. At others, there are hidden rocks. Face to face with an angry bear may come the racers at times. An exciting and dangerous race is the Iditarod.

_____

_____

_____

_____

_____

B. Revising Using a Variety of Sentence Orders

The writer of this paragraph decided always to use the traditional word order of subject before verb. Rewrite the paragraph, this time using a variety of sentences, including those arranged in the traditional order of subject before verb and those in which the verb comes before the subject.

> The Palio is a famous horse race. It is held each year in Siena, Italy. Seventeen districts called *contrade* are in the city. Not every district is lucky enough to compete. Only ten horses actually race. They run around a most unusual course. The course leads around the square in downtown Siena. The horses race around the course three times. The race is wild. No rules are set. About 70,000 people cheer excitedly. The winning horse is hugged after the race. Parties continue all night long.

_____

_____

_____

_____

_____

Lesson 6

Subject Complements

Reteaching

Complements are words that complete the meaning or action of verbs. **Subject complements** are words that follow a linking verb and identify or describe the subject.

Predicate adjectives are subject complements that describe or modify the subject.

The snow <u>was</u> <u>heavy</u>.
SUBJECT LINKING PREDICATE
         VERB   ADJECTIVE

Predicate nominatives are subject complements that are nouns or pronouns. They identify, rename, or define the subject.

The trip <u>became</u> <u>a nightmare</u>.
SUBJECT LINKING   PREDICATE
         VERB   ADJECTIVE

Identifying Linking Verbs and Subject Complements

In the following sentences, underline the linking verbs once and the subject complements twice.

1. All day the sky looked threatening.

2. People became nervous about the weather bulletins.

3. The chances for a major winter storm were excellent.

4. After all, blizzards are dangerous storms.

5. The roads became icy in early evening.

6. Television announcers sounded frantic.

7. The snow was light at first.

8. The major highways became sheets of ice.

9. Accumulations are the measurements of snow in inches.

10. Accumulations were highest near the lake.

11. Chardon and Chesterland were the sites of the most snow.

12. The winds were fierce.

13. The turnpike became impassable around two o'clock in the morning.

14. The next morning, schools were empty.

15. The outdoors became children's playgrounds.

16. Snacks of the day were hot chocolate and popcorn.

17. In people's homes, chocolate chip cookies smelled delicious.

18. The snow plows remained busy all day.

19. The winter storm warnings were only memories.

20. The winter sun looked pale in the light blue sky.

For use with Pupil's Edition pp. 50–51

Lesson 6

Subject Complements   *More Practice*

A. Identifying Types of Subject Complements

In each of the following sentences, underline the linking verb once and the subject complement twice. Then, in the blank, write **PN** if the subject complement is a predicate nominative or **PA** if it is a predicate adjective.

EXAMPLE Weather <u>is</u> the <u>state</u> of the atmosphere. *PN*

1. Hurricanes are especially dangerous storms.   _____

2. The eye of a hurricane is a calm area at the storm's center.   _____

3. The hurricane itself is an area of low air pressure.   _____

4. In the western Pacific region, the name for *hurricane* is *typhoon*.   _____

5. Hurricane tracking has become easier with modern equipment.   _____

6. Hurricane winds are extremely strong.   _____

7. These winds are often destructive.   _____

8. A hurricane's storm surge also becomes a major threat.   _____

9. The storm surge seems especially dangerous at high tide.   _____

10. Within the eye of the hurricane, the air stays calm.   _____

B. Using Subject Complements

Complete each sentence below. First complete it with a predicate nominative. Then complete it with a predicate adjective.

EXAMPLE The tornado was a *vicious storm*.
            The tornado was *frightening*.

1. The sky became _____.

The sky became _____.

2. The wind was _____.

The wind was _____.

3. Tornadoes are _____.

Tornadoes are _____.

4. After the tornado, our city was _____.

After the tornado, our city was _____.

5. The tornado's path was _____.

The tornado's path was _____.

Lesson 6

Subject Complements

Application

A. Writing Subject Complements

Rewrite each of the numbered items in the passage below with a new subject complement. Underline your new subject complement. If it is a predicate nominative, write **PN** in parentheses after the sentence. If it is a predicate adjective, write **PA.**

(1) The flooding of the Mississippi River in 1993 was a disaster. (2) Because of melting snows and heavy rains, the river became extremely high. (3) The situation was grim in river towns like St. Louis and Hannibal. (4) Rising water was a constant threat. (5) In the face of the disaster, residents were courageous. (6) In fact, many of them were heroes.

1. _____

2. _____

3. _____

4. _____

5. _____

6. _____

B. Writing with Subject Complements

Using words from the columns below, write six sentences with subject complements. You may use each word only once, and you must use all the words. You may change the form of the verb. Add other words to make your sentences interesting.

Nouns	Verbs	Adjectives
cloud	was	warm
weather	has become	inaccurate
sky	felt	threatening
forecast	is	dangerous
sun	looks	clear
drought	seems	unstable

1. _____

2. _____

3. _____

4. _____

5. _____

6. _____

For use with Pupil's Edition pp. 50–51

CHAPTER 2

Objects of Verbs

Reteaching

Sometimes action verbs require complements called direct objects and indirect objects to complete their meaning.

A **direct object** is a word or a group of words that receives the action of an action verb. A direct object answers the question *what* or *whom*.

> The class presented a <u>gift</u>. (The class presented *what?*)

Some sentences have both a direct object and an indirect object. An **indirect object** answers the question *to whom, for whom,* or *to what*. In a sentence with both kinds of objects, the indirect object always comes before the direct object.

> The class presented the <u>school</u> a gift. (*To whom* did the class present a gift?)

Recognizing Objects of Verbs

Write the direct object from each sentence below in the blank at the right. Then underline any indirect objects.

EXAMPLE Sonya read <u>us</u> a long story. *story*

1. Residents near this airport dislike the noise. _____

2. The plumber's assistant handed him a wrench. _____

3. Did the biology lab receive new equipment this year? _____

4. Robots are replacing people in some factories. _____

5. Mrs. White has been teaching students French for ten years. _____

6. The student council collected food for the homeless. _____

7. Did you write your aunt in Colorado a letter? _____

8. The Lee family gave the exchange students a welcoming party. _____

9. Carl Lewis won four gold medals in the 1984 Summer Olympics. _____

10. Judges presented the winner a silver trophy. _____

11. Rafael is making his sister a costume for the class party. _____

12. Jack, did you catch a trout at Pine Lake last week? _____

13. The inspector noticed the mud on the taxi driver's boot. _____

14. Some people took cameras to the air show. _____

15. Jen gave her cousin a framed picture for her birthday. _____

16. Mike sent his application to the summer program. _____

17. Did the mechanic inspect the brakes after the accident? _____

18. Will you save me a seat at the concert? _____

CHAPTER 2

GRAMMAR, USAGE, AND MECHANICS WORKBOOK **43**

Lesson 7

Objects of Verbs

More Practice

A. Identifying Objects of Verbs

Identify the function of the boldfaced word in each sentence below. Write **DO** for direct object and **IO** for indirect object. If the word is neither the direct object nor the indirect object, write **N**.

> **EXAMPLE** Cora writes **poetry** for the literary magazine. *DO*

1. The firefighters entered the **house** through the back door. _____

2. Mark sings in the adult **choir.** _____

3. The passenger left her **umbrella** behind on the bus. _____

4. The pianist played the **king** a beautiful sonata. _____

5. Alex paints **landscapes** in oil. _____

6. Gabi translated the **letter** from my pen pal in Germany. _____

7. The height of the steep cliff terrified **him.** _____

8. Paul told **us** the story of the phantom pirate ship. _____

9. Saul doesn't know about the committee's **decision.** _____

10. What gave **you** that idea? _____

B. Using Indirect Objects

Underline the direct object in each sentence below. Then rewrite each sentence, adding an indirect object. Use a different indirect object for every sentence.

1. My trip with Outward Bound last year taught self-confidence.

   _____

2. The salesclerk showed a new line of jewelry.

   _____

3. Grandmother brought a photograph of her as a young girl.

   _____

4. The waiter offered a menu.

   _____

5. The guide gave interesting information about the caverns.

   _____

For use with Pupil's Edition pp. 52–53

Name _____ Date _____

Lesson 7

Objects of Verbs

Application

A. Using Objects of Verbs

Choose one word from each list below to complete each sentence. Use each word only once. Each sentence should have both an indirect object and a direct object. If you wish, you can add words to make the sentences more interesting.

Use as indirect object	Use as direct object
students	snacks
passengers	greetings
surgeon	headache
Earthlings	roses
concertgoer	techniques
her	scalpel

1. The loud music gave _____.

2. Gina's boyfriend sent _____.

3. The swim coach taught _____.

4. The extraterrestrials brought _____.

5. The nurse handed _____.

6. The flight attendant offered _____.

B. Writing Sentences with Objects of Verbs

Complete each sentence with both an indirect object and a direct object.

EXAMPLE The mother bird brought *her babies a fat worm*.

1. The principal gave _____.

2. The batboy handed _____.

3. For her birthday, I made _____.

4. The gym teacher taught _____.

5. The webmaster sent _____.

6. The magician showed _____.

7. The toddler handed _____.

8. The gentleman offered _____.

9. The criminal told _____.

10. Our aunt wrote _____.

CHAPTER 2

Lesson 8

Sentence Diagramming

More Practice 1

Complete each diagram with the sentence provided.

A. Simple Subjects and Verbs

Dogs bark.

B. Compound Subjects and Verbs

Compound Subject Dogs and seals bark.

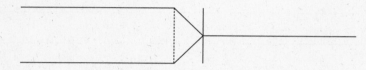

Compound Verb Dogs bark and growl.

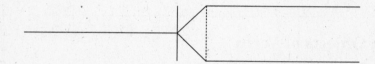

Compound Subject and Compound Verb Dogs and seals bark and growl.

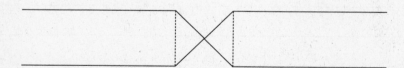

C. Adjectives and Adverbs

Adjectives and Adverbs Those small dogs are barking loudly.

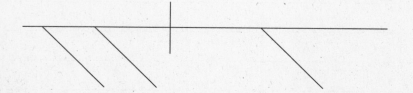

For use with Pupil's Edition pp. 54–57

Sentence Diagramming

More Practice 2

D. Subject Complements: Predicate Nominatives and Predicate Adjectives

Predicate Nominative That tall, thin dog is a saluki.

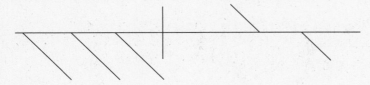

Predicate Adjective A saluki is very swift.

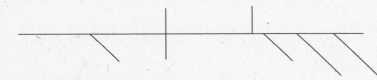

E. Direct Objects

Single Direct Object The saluki has a smooth, silky coat.

Compound Direct Object The judges rate appearance and behavior.

Compound Predicate The judges rate the dogs and then award prizes.

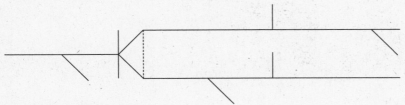

F. Indirect Objects

The judges have awarded that handsome saluki a prize.

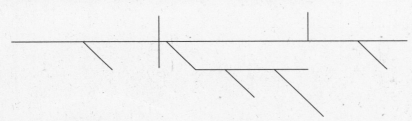

Sentence Diagramming

Application

On a separate piece of paper, diagram each of these sentences.

A. Diagramming Subjects, Verbs, and Modifiers

1. Dog owners often compete.
2. Their dogs usually behave well.
3. Three hundred dog breeds exist today.
4. Most young puppies develop quickly and learn easily.

B. Diagramming Subject Complements and Objects

1. The dog is mankind's oldest pet.
2. Dogs will often bury bones and food.
3. Some dogs are strong and can pull loads.
4. Training classes teach dogs useful skills.

C. Mixed Practice

1. Breeders have developed many modern breeds.
2. The Chihuahua is the smallest dog.
3. Newborn pups are helpless.
4. Pet dogs have often become heroes.
5. Dogs' best senses are smell and hearing.
6. Pets have sensed danger and have given their owners warnings.
7. Barks and yelps can be a clear language.
8. Dogs perceive little color.

For use with Pupil's Edition pp. 54–57

Prepositional Phrases

Reteaching

A **prepositional phrase** consists of a preposition, its object, and any modifiers of the object.

> Scientists observe stars <u>through a telescope</u>. (The preposition is *through*.)

An **adverb phrase** modifies a verb, an adjective, or another adverb.

> We see many stars <u>with the naked eye</u>. (The phrase modifies *see*, telling how.)

An **adjective phrase** modifies a noun or a pronoun.

> Light <u>from the stars</u> travels quickly. (The phrase modifies *light*, telling what kind.)

A. Identifying Prepositional Phrases

Underline the prepositional phrases in the following sentences.

> **EXAMPLE** Astronomers have made many discoveries <u>about the galaxy</u>.

1. Can anyone count the stars in the Milky Way?
2. The Milky Way looks beautiful on a clear night.
3. I enjoy stargazing from a nearby hilltop.
4. Clusters of stars form constellations.
5. Seven very bright stars surrounded by dust form the Seven Sisters.
6. Stars emit huge amounts of light.
7. Starlight passing through the atmosphere produces twinkling.
8. Stars change size, shape, and color in their life spans.
9. Different stars are fascinating to astronomers.
10. For centuries, people have looked into the heavens.

B. Identifying Words Modified by Prepositional Phrases

Underline the prepositional phrase in each of the following sentences once. Underline the word it modifies twice.

> **EXAMPLE** The quarterback <u>threw</u> the ball <u>into the end zone</u>.

1. Can you pronounce the name of the country?
2. The soprano sang one of my favorite songs.
3. In the cave an ancient artist had painted a hunting scene.
4. Along the path we planted pink and yellow tulips.
5. Can you see well in the dark?
6. The baseball flew over the fence.
7. Can you see that mountain in the distance?
8. The band played a song from a popular musical.
9. One of the hockey players was seriously injured.
10. During the storm all traffic stopped.

Prepositional Phrases

More Practice

A. Identifying Prepositional Phrases

Underline the prepositional phrase in each sentence. Write the word it modifies on the line.

1. Many stars together create cloudy bands of light. _____

2. Traveling clouds of dust are called nebulas. _____

3. Stars are formed from these nebulas. _____

4. Many stars in the sky died years ago. _____

5. Some stars are hidden behind dark nebulas. _____

6. Even astronomers cannot see these stars with powerful telescopes. _____

7. Star clusters held together by gravity are called galaxies. _____

8. Galaxies are found throughout the universe. _____

9. Alpha Centauri is the star closest to our solar system. _____

10. Scientists have many theories about star formation. _____

B. Identifying Prepositional Phrases as Modifiers

Underline the prepositional phrase in each sentence once. Underline the word it modifies twice. Then, in the blank, write **ADJ** or **ADV** to identify what kind of prepositional phrase it is.

EXAMPLE Many scientific <u>discoveries</u> are made <u>by chance</u>. _ADV_

1. Where would we be without creative geniuses? _____

2. Consider the wonders of modern medical science. _____

3. Hundreds of new drugs now prolong our lives. _____

4. Other inventions around the world have made life easier. _____

5. Pierre Verdon of France developed the food processor. _____

6. The microwave oven was invented in 1946. _____

7. Microwave ovens for the home came much later, however. _____

8. During the 1970s, the first home video games were sold. _____

9. Compare them to today's challenging games. _____

10. With their high-tech graphics, today's video games are entertaining. _____

11. Imagine life today without the personal computer. _____

12. Its invention in 1978 revolutionized technology. _____

For use with Pupil's Edition pp. 66–68

Lesson 1

Prepositional Phrases

Application

A. Using Prepositional Phrases as Modifiers

Revise the sentences below, adding prepositional phrases to modify the words that are italicized.

EXAMPLE I read a ***book.***
I read a book about great inventions.

1. The first stone ***tools*** begin the story of invention.

_____

2. Archaeologists can provide ***clues.***

_____

3. To find these clues, archaeologists ***looked.***

_____

4. Perhaps the greatest ***invention*** was the wheel.

_____

5. With the wheel, people ***could move*** heavy loads.

_____

6. The ***people*** probably found survival difficult.

_____

B. Writing with Prepositional Phrases

Write sentences using the following prepositional phrases. Then underline the words the phrases modify.

1. of all time

_____

2. by the teacher's desk

_____

3. after the fireworks

_____

4. with great care

_____

5. across the river

_____

CHAPTER 3

Appositives and Appositive Phrases

Reteaching

An **appositive** is a noun or pronoun that identifies or renames another noun or pronoun.

> The name <u>George</u> has been popular for generations. (*George* identifies *name*.)

An **appositive phrase** consists of an appositive plus its modifiers.

> George Washington, <u>our first president</u>, was considered quite tall.

A. Identifying Appositives and Appositive Phrases

Underline the appositive or appositive phrase in the following sentences.

1. Washington was awkward with women until he met his wife-to-be, Martha Custis.
2. No salary was paid to President Washington, our country's first millionaire.
3. He did not live in the White House, today's executive mansion, because it was not built until John Adams's administration.
4. Thomas Jefferson, author of the Declaration of Independence, was extremely well educated.
5. He was a gifted architect who designed Monticello, his home in Virginia.
6. Jefferson admired the work of Italian architect Andrea Palladio.
7. Jefferson's most significant achievement, the Louisiana Purchase, doubled the size of the United States.
8. At only 100 pounds, James Madison, our fourth president, was sickly throughout his life.
9. President John Quincy Adams kept an unusual pet, an alligator.
10. Andrew Jackson led the nation to a great victory, the Battle of New Orleans.
11. At his infamous inaugural party, a boisterous riot, Jackson fled for his life.
12. He was the only president ever to kill a man, a scoundrel, in a duel.
13. William Henry Harrison, a long-winded speaker, caught pneumonia while delivering his inaugural speech.
14. His early death caused him to have the shortest term of all the presidents, only one month.
15. President Zachary Taylor grazed his horse, Old Whitey, on the White House lawn.

B. Identifying Appositives and Appositive Phrases and Their Role

Underline the appositive or appositive phrase in the following sentences. Underline twice the word that the appositive or appositive phrase renames or identifies.

1. Franklin Pierce had dark, curly hair, his one outstanding physical feature.
2. James Buchanan relied on his niece Harriet as his official hostess.
3. Young Abraham Lincoln, a gangling boy, was largely self-educated.
4. While in the White House, Lincoln was saddened by death of his son Willie.
5. Of all his children, only Lincoln's son Robert lived to adulthood.

For use with Pupil's Edition pp. 69–70

Lesson 2

Appositives and Appositive Phrases

More Practice

A. Identifying Appositive Phrases

Underline the appositive or appositive phrase in each sentence. Write the noun it identifies on the blank line.

EXAMPLE Lincoln, <u>a lawyer from Illinois</u>, lost many elections. *Lincoln*

1. A unique storyteller, Abraham Lincoln was known for his wit. _____

2. Lincoln, a good listener, learned from other people. _____

3. He was a good father to his three sons, Robert, Willie, and Tad. _____

4. The Lincoln boys had a pet turkey, Jack. _____

5. Lincoln gave his famous speech, the *Gettysburg Address*, at the dedication of the cemetery at Gettysburg, Pennsylvania. _____

6. His great achievement, the Emancipation Proclamation, made slavery illegal. _____

B. Using Appositives and Appositive Phrases

Rewrite each of the following sentences, adding the appositive phrase shown in parentheses. Use commas if necessary.

1. Ulysses S. Grant was surprisingly gentle with people and animals. (a military genius)

_____

2. Grant was praised as the man most responsible for the Union victory in the Civil War. (a graduate of West Point)

_____

3. President Grant is buried in New York City. (the largest city on the East Coast)

_____

4. President Theodore Roosevelt read Kenneth Grahame's book to his children often. (*The Wind in the Willows*)

_____

5. Roosevelt became the namesake of one of America's favorite toys. (the teddy bear)

_____

6. Presidential cow lived on the White House grounds during William H. Taft's term of office. (Mooly Wooly)

_____

7. Taft once got stuck in the bathtub. (an extremely large man)

_____

CHAPTER 3

Lesson 2

Appositives and Appositive Phrases   *Application*

A. Writing with Appositives and Appositive Phrases

Combine the following sentences using an appositive or appositive phrase. Use commas as they are needed.

1. Franklin D. Roosevelt was the only child of a wealthy couple. He was elected president four times.

_____

2. He inspired the American people by speaking on the radio. The radio was the latest technological achievement at that time.

_____

3. Americans everywhere listened to these speeches. The speeches were called his "fireside chats."

_____

4. Though busy as president, Franklin Roosevelt found time for hobbies. He enjoyed working on his stamp albums and building models of ships.

_____

5. Eleanor Roosevelt represented the United States in the United Nations. She was the niece of Theodore Roosevelt and wife of Franklin Roosevelt.

_____

B. Using Appositives and Appositive Phrases

You have been elected president of your class. Write a short paragraph describing the goals you have and the people you need to help you accomplish them. Use at least five appositives or appositive phrases in your sentences. Underline the appositives and appositive phrases in your paragraph.

_____

_____

_____

_____

_____

_____

_____

_____

For use with Pupil's Edition pp. 69–70

CHAPTER 3

Verbals—Participial Phrases

Reteaching

A **verbal** is a word that is a verb form but acts as a different part of speech.
A **participle** is a verbal that acts as an adjective and modifies a noun or pronoun.

A <u>waving</u> flag caught my eye. (The present participle *waving* modifies *flag*.)

<u>Surprised</u>, I blinked in disbelief. (The past participle *Surprised* modifies *I*.)

A **participial phrase** consists of a participle plus its modifiers and complements.

<u>Waving my hand to the bus driver</u>, I ran toward the stop. (The participial phrase *Waving my hand to the bus driver* modifies *I*.)

<u>Surprised by my sudden arrival</u>, the driver braked sharply. (The participial phrase *Surprised by my sudden arrival* modifies *driver*.)

A. Identifying Participles and Participial Phrases

In each sentence, find a participle or participial phrase that modifies the underlined noun or pronoun. Underline the participle or participial phrase.

1. Increased <u>demand</u> for food is the result of the growth in the world's population.
2. The popular comedian bowed to the laughing <u>audience</u>.
3. The <u>doctor</u> examining me ordered a blood test.
4. Soothed by the music, <u>Kevin</u> fell asleep in his chair.
5. In the film about endangered <u>species</u>, I saw a bald eagle.
6. Tired after the long practice, the <u>athlete</u> stumbled.
7. Packing hurriedly, <u>Tara</u> forgot her shoes.
8. We frantically bailed water from the flooded <u>basement</u>.
9. <u>Andrea</u>, leaping several feet into the air, caught the softball.
10. A baked <u>potato</u> comes with every meal.

B. Identifying Participles and Participial Phrases

Underline the participle or participial phrase in each sentence. Underline twice the word that the participle or participial phrase modifies.

1. Taken for granted by most of us, paper is an essential part of our lives.
2. The paper used today has developed over many centuries.
3. Ancient Egyptians wrote on a sheet formed from stalks of a reed.
4. The reed, called *papyrus,* grew along the Nile River.
5. Cut down, the reed stalks were sliced into thin strips.
6. Can you imagine the laborers working in the hot sun?
7. The papyrus strips, laid in crisscross layers, were pressed together into fairly smooth sheets.
8. Modern paper, however, started with a Chinese inventor serving Emperor He Di.
9. The inventor's name was Cai Lun, also spelled Ts'ai Lun.
10. Arabs fighting near China's borders captured Chinese papermakers and brought their art to the West.

Verbals—Participial Phrases

More Practice

A. Identifying Participles and Participial Phrases

Underline the participle or participial phrase in each sentence. On the blank at the right, write the word that the participle or participial phrase modifies.

1. The tailor repaired my ripped jacket in just a few minutes. _____

2. A motorist driving recklessly through the town was arrested. _____

3. The book told about actual buried treasure in the United States. _____

4. Using combinations of leaves and stems, the Japanese make artful arrangements. _____

5. That extravagantly bound book is a first edition of *Treasure Island.* _____

6. The Founding members of our nation showed great foresight. _____

7. James finally found his gym socks, stuffed into a corner of his dresser drawer. _____

8. The Cullinan, having a weight of 3,024 carats in its rough state, is the world's largest diamond. _____

9. Fred, observing state law, switched on the car headlights as the rain began. _____

10. The scraping sound from outdoors was being made by a snowplow. _____

B. Identifying Dangling and Misplaced Participial Phrases

Underline the participial phrase in each sentence. Underline twice the word that the participial phrase modifies, if it exists. If the participial phrase is used correctly in the sentence, write **Correct** on the line at the right. If the phrase is placed incorrectly, write **Misplaced.** If there is no word modified by the phrase, write **Dangling.**

1. A few years ago, forecasters predicting the future talked about a "paperless office." _____

2. Office workers using computers supposedly would not handle papers. _____

3. Recalling these predictions, more paper than ever is needed now. _____

4. We can revise documents in a few minutes written on the computer. _____

5. Then, striking a single key, our printers churn out dozens of pages. _____

6. Wasted by our reliance on computers, we throw away mounds of paper. _____

7. Avoiding further waste of resources, waste paper is recycled in many offices. _____

8. In the garage of an office building, you might find a huge container filled four feet deep with paper. _____

For use with Pupil's Edition pp. 71–73

Verbals—Participial Phrases

Application

A. Using Participles and Participial Phrases

Write a sentence for each of the following participles and participial phrases. Use a comma after each participial phrase that begins a sentence. Then underline the word the participles or participial phrases modify.

1. watching the television _____

_____

2. pictured _____

_____

3. calling a friend _____

_____

4. confused _____

_____

5. leaving the mail on the table_____

_____

B. Using Participial Phrases in Writing

Combine the following pairs of sentences, using the boldfaced word to form a participial phrase. Use a comma after each participial phrase that begins a sentence.

1. Japanese paper folding is **known** as origami. Japanese paper folding is of two kinds: traditional and creative.

_____

_____

2. Traditional origami **calls** for folding colored paper into simple figures such as a butterfly or frog. It has the greatest appeal for children.

_____

_____

3. Creative origami is used to make original, complex figures. Creative origami **requires** cutting, combining, and pasting.

_____

_____

Lesson 4

Verbals—Gerund Phrases

Reteaching

A **gerund** is a verbal that ends in *–ing* and acts as a noun.

> <u>Walking</u> puts less stress on your legs than <u>running</u>.

A **gerund phrase** consists of a gerund plus its modifiers and complements.

> Roger Bannister won fame by <u>running the mile in less than four minutes</u>.

In sentences, gerunds and gerund phrases may be used anywhere nouns may be used.

As subject	<u>Walking</u> is my favorite exercise.
As predicate nominative	My favorite exercise is <u>walking</u>.
As direct object	I enjoy <u>walking a mile a day</u>.
As object of a preposition	I control my weight by <u>walking a mile each day</u>.
As indirect object	You should give <u>walking</u> a try.

A. Identifying Gerunds and Gerund Phrases

In each sentence, underline every gerund phrase once. Underline each gerund twice.

1. A catamaran is a sailboat made by joining two separate hulls together.
2. Leaving a little space between the two hulls is important.
3. Natives of the South Seas invented the "cat" by tying two logs together.
4. Using paddles and sometimes sails made the "cats" go very fast.
5. People who ride on a "cat" enjoy skimming over the water and attracting the attention of curious onlookers.
6. Jim's goal for the summer is building a catamaran of his own.

B. Identifying Gerunds and Gerund Phrases

Underline each gerund or gerund phrase. On the blank, write how it is used: **S** for subject, **PN** for predicate nominative, **DO** for direct object, or **OP** for object of a preposition.

1. Cheering the team gave me a sore throat. _____

2. Joanna's mother enjoys preserving fruits and vegetables. _____

3. We stopped him from telling the secret. _____

4. Alicia's worst fashion habit is wearing her sweater inside out. _____

5. Playing chess takes a great deal of concentration. _____

6. One of the more dangerous sports is skiing down almost-vertical slopes. _____

7. Mr. Karl doesn't approve of coming late. _____

8. Thank you for listening to my explanation. _____

9. To get rid of the skunk odor, try washing the dog with tomato juice. _____

10. Hearing the wind moan scared the children. _____

For use with Pupil's Edition pp. 74–75

CHAPTER 3

Lesson 4

Verbals—Gerund Phrases   *More Practice*

A. Identifying Gerunds and Gerund Phrases

Underline each gerund or gerund phrase. In the blank, write how it is used: **S** for
subject, **PN** for predicate nominative, **DO** for direct object, or **OP** for object of a
preposition.

1. Eating tomatoes hardly seems a daring act today, but tomatoes were once
   thought to be poisonous.   _____

2. Thomas Jefferson could count growing the first tomato in the United States
   among his accomplishments.   _____

3. Many people, by believing the tomato poisonous, slowed its acceptance. _____

4. People eventually started appreciating the tomato's value.   _____

5. Although the tomato is no longer considered harmful, some doubt still exists
   about classifying it as a fruit or a vegetable.   _____

6. Labeling it as a fruit seemed logical to botanists.   _____

7. Yet using a fruit in soups and sauces seemed strange to nonscientists. _____

8. The controversy continued, and eventually the Supreme Court was faced
   with deciding the issue.   _____

9. The Court's problem was satisfying both the scientific and the nonscientific
   worlds.   _____

10. In 1893 the Court solved the problem by classifying the tomato as a vegetable
    for purposes of trade only.   _____

B. Using Gerunds and Gerund Phrases

Rewrite each sentence. Change the boldfaced word or words to a gerund or
gerund phrase, and underline the gerund or gerund phrase. You may need to alter
some other words in the sentence.

1. **To sail** has always appealed to me.

   _____

2. My long-term project has been **to find a patient teacher.**

   _____

3. My misfortune is **to be a total klutz.**

   _____

4. **To stay out of the way of the sail** is impossible for me.

   _____

5. All I can aim for is **to be allowed on a sailboat as a guest.**

   _____

Verbals—Gerund Phrases

Application

A. Using Gerunds and Gerund Phrases

Write sentences using the following gerunds and gerund phrases in the sentence parts indicated.

1. crossing an ocean (subject) _____

_____

2. feeding the crew (object of preposition) _____

_____

3. watching the sun set (predicate nominative) _____

_____

4. feeling the boat rock (direct object) _____

_____

5. seeing strange, new lands (your choice of position) _____

_____

B. Using Gerunds and Gerund Phrases in Writing

You are applying for a job at a beach resort. The openings you are qualified for include these: cashier at the gift shop, waitperson at the restaurant, counterperson at the snack shop, childcare worker at the daycare center, lifeguard, and crew member on the ferryboat or the glass-bottom boat. (All of them pay the same hourly rate.) Write a paragraph identifying which job you would like best and why you should be chosen. Use five or more gerunds in your statement.

_____

_____

_____

_____

_____

_____

_____

_____

_____

Verbals—Infinitive Phrases

Reteaching

An **infinitive** is a verbal that usually begins with the word *to* and acts as a noun, an adjective, or an adverb. In each example below, the infinitive is *to be*. An **infinitive phrase** consists of an infinitive plus its complements and modifiers.

As noun <u>To be a recording star</u> sounds exciting. (subject of sentence)
Trina wants <u>to be a recording star</u>. (direct object)
Trina's wish is <u>to be a recording star</u>. (predicate nominative)

As adjective A desire <u>to be famous</u> is natural. (to be *famous* modifies *desire*)

As adverb <u>To be successful</u>, Trina will need luck as well as talent and drive.
(*To be successful* modifies *will need,* telling why.)

A. Identifying Infinitives

Underline the infinitive in each sentence.

1. Bill's goal is to become a psychiatrist someday.
2. Local patriots decided to throw the tea into the harbor.
3. Who wants to go with me to the game?
4. Paramedics arrived and tried to revive the victim.
5. Tony worked to earn money for a bicycle.
6. Paula would like to learn some Spanish before her trip to Mexico.
7. The umpire stopped to clean home plate.
8. To save time, playwright George Bernard Shaw learned shorthand.
9. To listen well is an important skill.
10. The manager of the team didn't want to miss the kickoff.

B. Identifying Infinitive Phrases

Underline the infinitive phrase in each sentence. On the blank, write how it is used:
N for noun, **ADJ** for adjective, or **ADV** for adverb.

1. To understand the difference between a democracy and a republic is important. _____

2. The captain struggled to regain control of the foundering ship. _____

3. The political prisoner refused to denounce his principles. _____

4. Magellan's ship was the first to circumnavigate the globe. _____

5. The class approved the decision to offer tutoring services to younger children. _____

6. Kara's plan is to take a trip to Australia next year. _____

7. The hill above the town is the best place to watch the fireworks. _____

8. Prospective team members must promise to attend regular practice sessions. _____

Lesson 5

Verbals—Infinitive Phrases

More Practice

A. Identifying Infinitive Phrases

Underline the infinitive phrase in each sentence. On the blank, write how it is used:
N for noun, **ADJ** for adjective, or **ADV** for adverb.

1. To get rich quickly is a dream for many people. _____

2. A few people act to make that dream come true. _____

3. About 100 years ago, the chance to strike it rich appeared in Alaska. _____

4. A few prospectors brave enough to explore the frozen interior found gold
   in the summer of 1896. _____

5. The first lucky adventurers hoped to stake their claims before word reached
   the outside world. _____

6. They had good reasons to worry about losing their opportunity. _____

7. When the first ship to carry gold out of Alaska reached Seattle the following
   summer, news of the discovery spread like wildfire. _____

8. People from all over the world spent all their savings to make their way to Alaska. _____

9. Unfortunately, to come late to a gold rush guarantees disappointment. _____

10. A few people made fortunes and left wealthy; others learned to love Alaska
    and stayed, with or without gold. _____

B. Using Infinitive Phrases

Use each of the following infinitive phrases in a sentence.

1. to revive the victim speedily

_____

2. to arrange flowers attractively

_____

3. to provide a good target for the baseball pitcher

_____

4. to swim in the Olympics

_____

5. to explore the depths of the ocean

_____

For use with Pupil's Edition pp. 76–77

CHAPTER 3

Lesson 5

Verbals—Infinitive Phrases

Application

A. Using Infinitive Phrases

Use each of the following infinitive phrases in a sentence.

1. to become fluent in French

_____

2. to recall the year of the blizzard

_____

3. to write a best seller

_____

4. to avoid burning the toast

_____

5. to earn money for college

_____

B. Writing Infinitive Phrases

Rewrite each pair of sentences as a single sentence by changing the underlined sentence to an infinitive phrase within the other sentence.

EXAMPLE 1 I will read a book each week. That is my plan.
REVISION 1 *To read a book each week is my plan.* or
My plan is to read a book each week.

EXAMPLE 2 Gail suggested, "Let's have a party." We liked her suggestion.
REVISION 2 *We liked Gail's suggestion to have a party.*

EXAMPLE 3 Frank waited for a sale on jackets. Then he could save money.
REVISION 3 *To save money, Frank waited for a sale on jackets.*

1. My family has made a decision. We will go to Alaska for two weeks.

_____

2. We will see the midnight sun. That is what I want most.

_____

3. We've made the arrangements. We used our computer.

_____

4. We will leave for the airport very early. We will board our flight at 6 A.M.

_____

5. I will have trouble sleeping with the sky light all night. I expect this will be true.

_____

CHAPTER 3

Lesson 6

Placement of Phrases

Reteaching

Writers can easily confuse readers by placing a prepositional, participial, or infinitive phrase in the wrong position in a sentence. A **misplaced phrase** is a phrase that appears to modify a word other than the one the writer intended it to modify.

> **EXAMPLE** Hiking in the hot sun, we thought of shoveling snow <u>with longing</u>.
> (Did the speaker shovel snow with longing?)

> **REVISION** Hiking in the hot sun, we thought <u>with longing</u> of shoveling snow.

A **dangling phrase** is a phrase that is intended to modify a word that does not appear in the sentence.

> **EXAMPLE** Walking to town, the twisted signpost was confusing. (Who was walking? It was certainly not the signpost!)

> **REVISION** Walking to town, we were confused by the twisted signpost.

Sometimes, as in the second example, you will need to change the voice of the verb in order to bring the phrase close to the word it should modify.

A. Finding the Words Modified by Misplaced Phrases

Each underlined phrase is misplaced. On the line at the right, write the word that the phrase was intended to modify.

1. The forest ranger spotted a distant bear <u>using high-powered binoculars</u>. _____

2. Mrs. Diaz left the house <u>covered in fur</u>. _____

3. The actor rehearsed his part in the theater <u>with great emotion</u>. _____

4. Tom swatted the mosquito <u>muttering quietly</u>. _____

5. <u>With bright feathers</u>, Betsy watched the birds in the huge cage. _____

6. Patrick built a house for the dog <u>made of wood</u>. _____

B. Identifying Misplaced and Dangling Phrases

Underline the misplaced or dangling phrase in each of the following sentences.

1. Opening the front door, snow was falling at a great rate.

2. The boy stopped at the stop sign on a bike.

3. To avoid hearing loss, the neighborhood should not hear your car radio.

4. All the players complained about the heat in the gym on Raisa's team.

5. Eating half a grapefruit, toast, and cereal for breakfast, Fred's day was off to a good start.

6. The new pediatric unit accepts all patients built with the aid of a grant.

7. Mowing the lawn, a nest of wasps was disturbed by Jennifer.

8. The children noticed the broken branch playing in the yard.

9. To hear the sound track for that comedy, it must be the funniest show on television.

10. Jogging along the woodland path, a moose was spied by Andy.

CHAPTER 3

Lesson 6

Placement of Phrases

More Practice

Correcting Misplaced and Dangling Phrases

If a sentence contains a misplaced or dangling phrase, rewrite it to eliminate the error. If the sentence is correct, write **Correct.**

1. Ramon saw an airplane walking home.

_____

2. Liking the color red, Arthur's new car is a brilliant flamingo.

_____

3. The cameraman filmed the lightning flashing in the sky.

_____

4. Ellie was driven to the clinic by a teammate holding ice to her forehead.

_____

5. Ask the customers to stand in a line waiting for rain checks for the new video.

_____

6. To win, the gymnast needs a score of 9.785.

_____

7. Riding in the country in the early spring, the air was so refreshing.

_____

8. To carry bulky packages on the bus, they should be tied together.

_____

9. We heard the sound of thunder sitting on the porch.

_____

10. A baby is in the carriage wrapped in blankets.

_____

11. Slamming the door behind him, my brother left the house.

_____

12. To find the right store, the mall has a map near the main entrance.

_____

13. The red coat belongs to Leela in the front closet.

_____

14. Living on land and in the sea, prehistoric times had gigantic creatures that were larger than any animal alive today.

_____

CHAPTER 3

Placement of Phrases

Application

A. Recognizing Misplaced Phrases

As a newspaper reader, what would you expect to read about in each of the articles described by the following headline and capsule summaries? For each item, write a humorous paragraph that builds on the absurd situation suggested by the misplaced phrase.

1. Divers Recover Cargo for Historical Society of Ancient Merchants

_____

_____

_____

2. We hear from the teen attacked by a bear entering City College.

_____

_____

_____

3. Try this cheesecake from a prize-winning cook covered with cherry sauce!

_____

_____

_____

4. To bring presents, children expect Santa's visit.

_____

_____

_____

B. Correcting Misplaced Phrases

Revise each of the headlines in Exercise A, moving the misplaced phrase so that the sentence has the meaning the writer actually intended.

1. _____

2. _____

3. _____

4. _____

For use with Pupil's Edition pp. 78–79

Sentence Diagramming   *More Practice 1*

A. Prepositional Phrases

Adjective Phrases An editor of the *Pittsburgh Dispatch* wrote an editorial against women at work.

Adverb Phrases This editorial was printed in 1895.

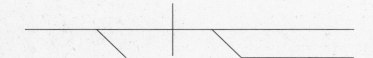

B. Appositive Phrases

Elizabeth Cochrane, one of the paper's readers, wrote an indignant response.

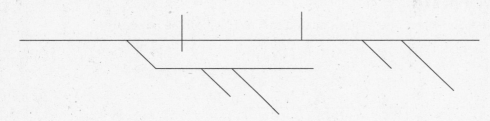

C. Participial Phrases

Attacking that editorial, so patronizing toward women, Elizabeth defended women's abilities.

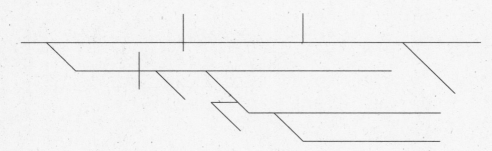

Sentence Diagramming

More Practice 2

D. Gerund Phrases

Gerund Phrase as Subject Writing that letter changed Elizabeth's life.

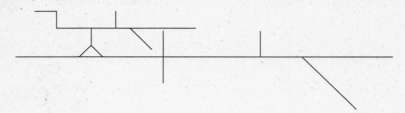

Gerund Phrase as Object of Preposition She succeeded in getting the editor's attention.

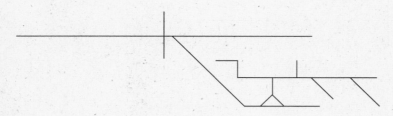

E. Infinitive Phrases

Infinitive Phrase as Object The editor decided to hire Elizabeth as a reporter.

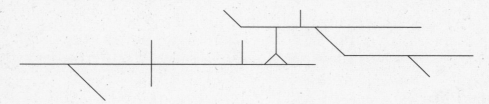

Infinitive Phrase as Adverb Elizabeth worked hard to prove her ability.

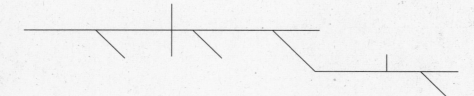

For use with Pupil's Edition pp. 80–83

Sentence Diagramming

Application

On a separate piece of paper, diagram each of these sentences.

A. Diagramming Prepositional, Appositive, and Participial Phrases

1. In her writing, Elizabeth Cochrane used the name Nellie Bly.
2. The name came from a song by Stephen Foster, the famous American composer.
3. Nellie wrote articles describing the hard lives of the poor.
4. Communicating her own concern for others, Nellie aroused readers' sympathy for poor working women.

B. Diagramming Gerund Phrases and Infinitive Phrases

1. After winning loyal readers, Nellie was given an unusual assignment.
2. In those days, traveling in foreign countries was dangerous for a single woman.
3. Nellie went to Mexico to report on life in that country.
4. Reading her articles helped stay-at-homes to imagine a different culture.

C. Mixed Practice

1. To get more excitement, Nellie then moved to a New York newspaper.
2. Her first assignment was pretending to be insane.
3. Admitted to an insane asylum, Nellie stayed for two weeks to get the facts about conditions inside.
4. Her articles reporting on abuse of patients resulted in action to improve their treatment.
5. In her most famous exploit, Nellie tried to travel around the world in 80 days.
6. She got the idea from reading the popular novel *Around the World in 80 Days*.
7. Riding ships, trains, and mules, Nellie raced to beat the hero of Jules Verne's novel.
8. Completing the trip in only 72 days brought Nellie worldwide fame.

Kinds of Clauses

Reteaching

A **clause** is a group of words that contains both a subject and a verb. An **independent** (or **main**) clause expresses a complete thought and forms a sentence.

> The summer <u>months</u> <u>bring</u> their own sounds.
>   SUBJECT   VERB

A **subordinate** (or **dependent**) **clause** contains a subject and a verb but does not express a complete thought. It cannot stand alone as a sentence. Subordinate clauses are often introduced by such words as *if, because, even though, how, what, why, that, when, while,* and *since.*

> when the <u>temperature</u> <u>rises</u> (What happens at this time?)
>   SUBJECT   VERB

A subordinate clause must always be combined with, or be part of, an independent clause.

> <u>When the temperature rises</u>, <u>insects get noisy</u>.
>   SUBORDINATE CLAUSE   INDEPENDENT CLAUSE

A verbal phrase does not have a subject and is not the same as a subordinate clause.

> <u>Chattering at birds</u>, squirrels raise a fuss. (verbal phrase)
> <u>When <u>they</u> are chattering at birds</u>, squirrels raise a fuss. (subordinate clause)

A. Identifying Subordinate Clauses and Verbal Phrases

Identify each boldfaced group of words by writing **SC** for a subordinate clause and **VP** for a verbal phrase.

1. Locusts are some of the noisiest insects **that live in this part of the country.** _____

2. When locusts rub their hind legs against their wings, they make a sound. _____

3. To listen to locusts on a hot summer night can be pleasant. _____

4. Have you heard the sound **that they make?** _____

5. Locusts are louder, **but hornets are more threatening.** _____

6. Hearing the buzz of a hornet, I start running. _____

B. Identifying Independent and Subordinate Clauses

Identify each boldfaced group of words by writing **IND** for independent clause and **SUB** for subordinate clause.

1. The fans felt **that their team's victory was impressive.** _____

2. Robin planted a wide variety of flowers in her garden. _____

3. Melanie, **who is a very cheerful person,** has many friends. _____

4. Pam arrived at the party early and stayed late, **but Frank arrived late and left early.** _____

5. Suzanne can't play basketball **because she sprained her wrist.** _____

For use with Pupil's Edition pp. 92–93

Lesson 1

Kinds of Clauses

More Practice

A. Identifying Independent and Subordinate Clauses

Identify each boldfaced group of words by writing **IND** for independent clause and **SUB** for subordinate clause.

1. During summer in each hemisphere, the number of hours of daylight increases **because that part of the earth tilts toward the sun.** _____

2. At the equator, there is not much change, **but at the poles the difference is remarkable.** _____

3. As you go farther north, **the number of daylight hours in June grows.** _____

4. However, the speed **at which summer departs also increases.** _____

5. **During summer, most teenagers have more time for the things** that they want to do. _____

6. **Because Rina wanted to earn some extra money,** she applied for a part-time job in a local hardware store. _____

7. **Rina described her previous jobs** when the interviewer asked about her sales experience. _____

8. If Rina can work at least 20 hours a week, **the owner will give her a job.** _____

9. **After she finished her interview at the hardware store,** Rina called her mother. _____

10. Rina's neighbor was the one **who suggested applying at the store.** _____

B. Identifying Independent and Subordinate Clauses

Each sentence contains two clauses. In the blanks provided, identify each clause as independent or subordinate by writing **IND + IND, IND + SUB, or SUB + IND.**

1. The female sea turtle lays her eggs in the sand, and she selects a sunny place for the nest. _____

2. When she finds a place, she digs a hole about as deep as her hind limbs and deposits her eggs. _____

3. Several clutches can be laid, and each clutch can consist of 200 eggs. _____

4. Because the nests are carefully constructed, the whole process can take a few hours. _____

5. The incubation period varies since it depends on the temperature. _____

6. After the eggs are buried, the mother returns to the sea. _____

7. Since the mother has no interest in her eggs or hatchlings, the nests are often preyed upon by large birds and small mammals. _____

8. Although the hatchlings may reach the water, predaceous fish await to eat them. _____

CHAPTER 4

Kinds of Clauses

Application

A. Using Subordinate Clauses in Writing

Add an independent clause to each of the following subordinate clauses to create a complete sentence. Write your new sentences on the lines.

1. while the waves rose higher

_____

2. although he didn't say so

_____

3. because I have allergic reactions

_____

4. what they saw that night

_____

5. since the store opened this morning

_____

6. as if she knew all the answers

_____

B. Revising

The following paragraph has no capitalization to mark sentence beginnings or end marks to indicate their endings. Insert a period after the last word of each sentence, and mark the first letter in each sentence with a triple underscore (≡), the proofreading symbol for capitalization. When you are finished, write the number of sentences that combine both an independent and a dependent clause.

Number of sentences with both an independent and a dependent clause: _____

I would never become a farmer because the job is too risky the farmer's success depends on the weather, and no one on Earth controls that in a small plot, a gardener can water the plants, but most farmers must wait for rains to water their fields even if the farmer irrigates, the water for irrigation comes from a reservoir on the farm, such as a pond during a drought, the pond may dry up and so will the plants when there's too much rain, the plants drown temperature is another major factor that the farmer can't control if freezing weather lingers too late in the spring or arrives too early in the fall, the year's crops can be lost think about the farmer's problems with wild animals and insects, too I can't imagine how I'd fight off a swarm of locusts attacking my fields no, I could never be a farmer I'm thankful that other people are brave enough to take on that job.

Lesson 2

Adjective and Adverb Clauses

Reteaching

An **adjective clause** is a subordinate clause that modifies a noun or pronoun. It usually follows the word(s) it modifies. Like adjectives, adjective clauses answer the questions *which one, what kind, how much,* or *how many.* They are introduced by **relative pronouns** (such as *who, whom, whose, that,* and *which*) and **relative adverbs** (such as *when, where,* and *why*).

> Vivian did her report on an animal <u>that</u> <u>she admires</u>. (Which animal?)

> The library <u>where</u> <u>she did her research</u> is open on Sundays. (Which library?)

An **essential adjective clause** provides information that is essential, or necessary, to identify the preceding noun or pronoun. A **nonessential adjective clause** provides additional, but not necessary, information about a noun or pronoun in a sentence in which the meaning is already clear. Use commas to set off a nonessential clause.

> The animal <u>that</u> <u>she researched</u> is the horse. (essential)

> The horse, <u>which</u> <u>lives in many lands</u>, has a long history. (nonessential)

When choosing between *that* and *which,* use *that* to introduce essential clauses and *which* to introduce nonessential clauses.

An **adverb clause** is a subordinate clause that modifies a verb, adjective, or adverb. It may come before or after the word(s) it modifies. Like adverbs, adverb clauses tell *where, why, how, when,* or *to what degree* something was done.

> <u>As</u> <u>she spoke</u>, her classmates listened. (When did they listen? Modifies verb)

> She spoke more enthusiastically <u>than</u> <u>she had ever spoken before</u>.
> (How enthusiastically? Modifies adverb)

Adverb clauses are usually introduced by **subordinating conjunctions** that relate the adverb to the word(s) it modifies. The following is a list of some common subordinating conjunctions.

after	as long as	before	so	until	where
although	as soon as	even though	than	when	while
as	as though	if	though	whenever	
as if	because	since	unless	wherever	

Identifying Adjective and Adverb Clauses

Underline the adjective or adverb clause once. Underline the word modified twice.

1. The horse and the cow are probably the best-known members of the *Ungulate* order, which consists of more than 200 species of hoofed animals.

2. In Central Asia, where the horse was first domesticated about 5,000 years ago, stirrups were introduced about A.D. 750.

3. Even though they are all quite similar, modern horse breeds are of two classes.

4. The light horse class includes those horses that are used for riding, driving, and racing.

5. As you might expect, the draft horse class includes strong work animals.

CHAPTER 4

Adjective and Adverb Clauses

More Practice

A. Identifying Adjective and Adverb Clauses and Introductory Words

In each sentence, underline the adjective or adverb clause once. Underline the word it modifies twice. On the line, write the relative pronoun or relative adverb that introduces the adjective clause or the subordinating conjunction that introduces the adverb clause.

EXAMPLE Club <u>members</u> <u>who came late</u> paid a fine. *who*

1. Mary Ellen Chase, who wrote a number of successful novels set in Maine, also became a writing instructor at Smith College. _____

2. The TV special was a study of domestic cats, whose habits are clearly similar to those of lions in the wild. _____

3. As long as you're going to the store, please buy more chips. _____

4. The temperature has dropped lower than the forecasters predicted. _____

5. Richie had no interest in music until the day he first saw a concert grand piano. _____

6. Both cats looked as if they had something to hide. _____

7. Laser beams have replaced the surgical knives that were once used for delicate operations such as eye surgery. _____

8. Since the family got a new car, she has asked to drive it to school. _____

9. Bring your application to any Registry of Motor Vehicles clerk who is on duty on the first floor of the State Office Building. _____

10. The Renaissance was a time when the arts flourished in Western Europe. _____

B. Identifying Essential Clauses

Underline the adjective clause in each of the following sentences. Write **ESS** to the right if the clause is an essential adjective clause, or write **NON** if it is a nonessential clause. Insert commas where they are needed.

1. The word *wuthering* which is a Yorkshire word means "blowing fiercely." _____

2. Athens is the city where the first modern Olympic Games were held. _____

3. The kind of plain yogurt that is most nutritious contains live bacteria. _____

4. Alice Liddell was the little girl who inspired *Alice's Adventures in Wonderland*. _____

5. The cardinal which is the state bird of Kentucky belongs to the finch family. _____

6. English, Nigeria's official language, is not the language that is most commonly used. _____

For use with Pupil's Edition pp. 94–97

Adjective and Adverb Clauses   *Application*

A. Using Essential and Nonessential Clauses in Writing

Combine each numbered pair of sentences to form one sentence containing an adjective clause that modifies the boldfaced word. If the clause is nonessential, add commas. If the clause is essential, do not add commas.

1. There go the **workers.** The workers are resurfacing our street.

_____

2. I found the **page.** The page was missing from my notebook.

_____

3. My favorite piece of **needlework** has been damaged. It took me months to complete.

_____

4. A Boston **artist** attracts many onlookers. He draws in chalk on pavements.

_____

5. **Yolanda** finally found our house. She hates to use a road map.

_____

B. Using Adverb Clauses

Rewrite each of the following sentences, adding an adverb clause that begins with the word in parentheses. If the clause comes at the beginning or the middle of the sentence, set it off with commas. If it comes and the end of the sentence, do not use commas.

1. The horse in the story lived in a small town. (Use *where.*)

_____

2. A young girl had talked her parents into buying the horse. (Use *because.*)

_____

_____

3. One day the horse was horse-napped. (Use *while.*)

_____

4. The girl was heartbroken. (Use *until.*)

_____

5. The thieves were caught. (Use *even though.*)

_____

6. The girl cried with happiness. (Use *after.*)

_____

Noun Clauses

Reteaching

A **noun clause** is a subordinate clause that is used in a sentence as a noun. Noun clauses may be used anywhere in a sentence that nouns can be used and serve the same function as a noun.

Subject	<u>Whether the defendant is guilty</u> is the question.
Direct Object	The plaintiff claims <u>that her landlord cheated her</u>.
Indirect Object	She gives <u>whoever listens</u> a long, sad story.
Predicate Nominative	The truth may be <u>what she says</u>.
Object of a Preposition	Don't be swayed by <u>how tearful she becomes</u>.

Usually, a noun clause is introduced by one of these words: a **subordinating conjunction,** such as *that, how, when, where, whether,* and *why;* or a **relative pronoun,** such as *what, whatever, who, whom, whoever, whomever, which,* and *whichever.* If no introductory word is used, you can still recognize a noun clause if the clause can be replaced in the sentence by *someone* or *something.*

Identifying Noun Clauses and Their Uses

Underline the noun clause in each sentence. Then, on the line, indicate how the noun clause is used: write **S** for subject, **DO** for direct object, **IO** for indirect object, **PN** for predicate nominative, or **OP** for object of a preposition.

1. The bailiff announced that the judge was entering the room. _____

2. Whoever committed the crime should be punished. _____

3. His alibi is that he was bowling that night. _____

4. The angry man gave whoever was in his way a push. _____

5. Most of the jurors were alarmed by how readily the witness changed her story. _____

6. Tuesday was when the crime spree began. _____

7. None of the witnesses noticed whether she arrived with her husband. _____

8. The clerk made a list of what was missing. _____

9. Why anyone turns to a life of crime is a puzzle to me. _____

10. To avoid capture, the thief hid under whatever was at hand. _____

11. Juries must give whichever person is charged the benefit of the doubt. _____

12. Which house they broke into depended on the vandals' mood at that moment. _____

13. What the prosecution claimed, the defense rejected. _____

14. The bank robbers gave whoever was in the lobby a minute to lie down. _____

15. A dependable getaway car was what they lacked. _____

16. The villainous witness supported whichever side paid him well. _____

17. That the defendant has a criminal past was kept from the jury. _____

For use with Pupil's Edition pp. 98–100

Lesson 3

Noun Clauses

More Practice

A. Identifying Noun Clauses and Their Uses

Underline the noun clause in each sentence. Then, on the line, indicate how the noun clause is used: write **S** for subject, **DO** for direct object, **IO** for indirect object, **PN** for predicate nominative, or **OP** for object of a preposition.

1. How global warming affects our planet is a matter of great concern. _____

2. We can offer whoever answers our ad a choice of interview dates. _____

3. Jeannie didn't know how she could break the bad news to the yearbook staff. _____

4. The employer gave a generous bonus to whoever had been with the company for over one year. _____

5. What pleased Alex most was that he would be at a beach for his vacation. _____

6. Jeff's opinion was that we should apologize. _____

7. No one could understand why Penny became so angry. _____

8. The author gave a description of what life was like in the Middle Ages. _____

9. Looking at the night sky, Isabel wondered when the next full moon would be. _____

10. Please tell whoever answers the news. _____

B. Using Noun Clauses

Revise each of the numbered sentences by replacing the underlined word with one of the lettered noun clauses. Write the revised sentences on the lines provided.

    a. who gets called to serve on a jury
    b. how much time she will serve
    c. where the crime occurred
    d. why the wrongdoer committed the crime
    e. who caused the hung jury

1. The jurors were taken to <u>the place</u>.

_____

2. The twelfth juror was <u>the person</u>.

_____

3. The police have a better chance of finding the criminal if they know <u>that</u>.

_____

4. <u>That</u> is a result of chance.

_____

5. The judge decides <u>that</u>.

_____

CHAPTER 4

Lesson 3

Noun Clauses

Application

A. Using Noun Clauses

Rewrite each numbered sentence by including a noun clause as directed in the parentheses. Underline the noun clause in each new sentence.

(1) Marc met quite a few people on his vacation and told each one about his job (IO). **(2)** He remembers clearly his first days on the job as a court reporter (DO). **(3)** His interest in his job has not been dulled by the fact that he has been in it for a long time (OP). **(4)** His main interest is the person on trial; he doesn't care who it is (PN). **(5)** Besides, anything that comes to trial involves some mystery (S).

1. _____

2. _____

3. _____

4. _____

5. _____

B. Writing with Noun Clauses

You are a trial lawyer in a civil case involving the events described below. You may represent either the plaintiff or the defendant. Write your opening speech to the jury in which you outline what you intend to prove in this trial. In your speech, include at least five sentences using noun clauses. Show at least three of the possible uses of noun clauses (subject, direct object, indirect object, predicate nominative, or object of a preposition).

Defendant borrowed plaintiff's motorbike, promising to return it by 6 P.M. Because of tornado warnings, defendant did not return bike on time. Plaintiff phoned defendant at 7 P.M. and insisted on getting bike back immediately. Returning the bike in bad weather, defendant skidded and crashed. Although defendant was unhurt, the bike was a total loss. Plaintiff is suing for cost of new motorbike.

_____

_____

_____

_____

_____

_____

_____

_____

CHAPTER 4

For use with Pupil's Edition pp. 98–100

Sentence Structure

Reteaching

A **simple sentence** consists of one independent clause and no subordinate clauses. Any part of the sentence, such as subject, verb, or object, may be compound.

> <u>You</u> and <u>I</u> enjoy <u>games</u> and <u>sports</u>. (compound subject, compound object)

A **compound sentence** consists of two or more independent clauses joined together. Any of these can be used to join independent clauses: a comma and coordinating conjunction; a semicolon; or a semicolon followed by a conjunctive adverb and comma.

> New games are produced every shopping season; **nevertheless,** many old games retain their popularity.

A **complex sentence** consists of one independent clause and one or more subordinate clauses.

> <u>Although new games are produced every shopping season</u>, many games <u>that have been around for generations</u> retain their popularity.

A **compound-complex sentence** consists of two or more independent clauses and one or more subordinate clauses.

> New games are produced every shopping season; **nevertheless,** many games <u>that have been around for generations</u> retain their popularity.

Identifying Kinds of Sentences

Identify each sentence below with **S** for simple, **CD** for compound, **CX** for complex, or **CC** for compound-complex.

1. Hangman is a word game that both children and adults play. _____

2. A modern variation of hangman has become a popular television show. _____

3. Chinese checkers is played with marbles; it is an easy game to learn. _____

4. The playing board is round and has a star-like design on it. _____

5. A game that is played on a checkerboard of 64 squares is called checkers in the United States, but it is called draughts in Great Britain. _____

6. The purpose of the game is to win your opponents' playing pieces by "jumping" over them with your pieces. _____

7. Checker-type games were played by the ancient Egyptians, Greeks, and Romans, but checkers as it is played in the United States dates back only to the 1500s. _____

8. Chess, which probably originated in India in the 600s, is still played throughout the world. _____

9. In chess, international rules govern the playing of the game, but in checkers, each nation has its own rules. _____

Lesson 4 Sentence Structure   *More Practice*

A. Identifying Kinds of Sentences

Identify each sentence below with **S** for simple, **CD** for compound, **CX** for complex, or **CC** for compound-complex.

1. One aspect of history that is rarely studied in school is how people played. _____

2. Horseshoe pitching is a game that may be traced to Roman soldiers of about A.D. 100. _____

3. Can you imagine soldiers in togas pitching horseshoes? _____

4. Ninepins must be at least several hundred years old, since the story "Rip Van Winkle" depicts colonial settlers playing it. _____

5. Children are still playing ring-around-a-rosy, and this is a game that dates back to medieval times. _____

6. It is thought that the game began about the time of the Black Death. _____

7. The apparently light and meaningless words of the rhyme recall a disastrous time. _____

8. The line "A pocket full of posies" sounds pretty, but it probably refers to the sweet-smelling flowers that people carried to cover the smell of death. _____

9. The *All* in "All fall down" are the people who fell victim to the plague. _____

10. Generations of soldiers have believed that strategies learned in board games help prepare commanders for battlefield decisions. _____

B. Using Different Kinds of Sentences

Combine each numbered sentence with the sentence that follows to make a compound, complex, or compound-complex sentence. Write the new sentence on the line provided. Label in parentheses the sentence type: **CD, CX,** or **CC.**

(1) Before 1900, a phone was always black. It had a straight cord. **(2)** The phone had no dial. Operators placed all calls. **(3)** A caller lifted the receiver and waited. The operator said, "Number, please." **(4)** There were no call-forwarding features, and there were no answering machines. There was little automation then.

1. _____

_____

2. _____

3. _____

_____

4. _____

_____

For use with Pupil's Edition pp. 101–103

CHAPTER 4

Sentence Structure

Application

A. Using Different Structures to Combine Sentences

Combine the ideas expressed in the simple sentences of this paragraph into no more than five sentences. In parentheses after each sentence, label what kind of sentence you used: **CP** for compound, **CX** for complex, or **CC** for compound-complex.

> Dominoes is the name of a game. It is played with small tiles. There are 28 tiles in a set. The tiles are small. They are flat. They are oblong. A line on the face of each tile divides the shape into two squares. Each square is marked with zero to six dots. To begin, players mix the tiles. Each player draws up to seven tiles. The first player lays down a tile. The second player must lay next to it a second tile. The second tile must have at least one matching square. The square must match a square on the first tile.

_____

_____

_____

_____

_____

_____

_____

B. Using Different Sentence Structures in Directions

Write a paragraph of directions for playing a board game, card game, or other popular game. Include at least one of each kind of sentence: simple, compound, complex, and compound-complex. Label in parentheses the sentence type: **S, CD, CX,** or **CC.**

_____

_____

_____

_____

_____

_____

_____

_____

Lesson 5 Sentence Diagramming

More Practice 1

A. Simple Sentences At 3:02 A.M. on Tuesday, August 17, 1999, a major earthquake struck northwestern Turkey.

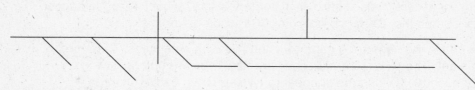

B. Compound Sentences The shaking lasted for 45 seconds, and thousands of buildings fell apart.

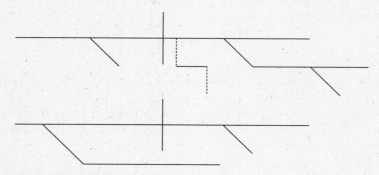

C. Complex Sentences
Adjective Clause Introduced by a Pronoun Yuksel Er, who had left his bed to go to the bathroom, was trapped in the debris of his apartment.

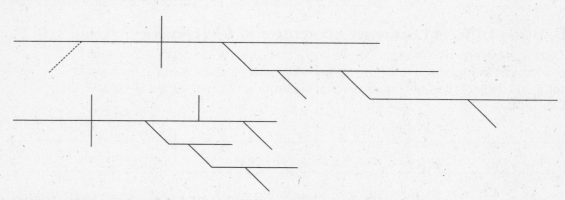

Adjective Clause Introduced by an Adverb The space where he lay for the next four days was the size of a coffin.

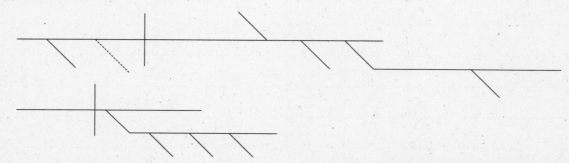

For use with Pupil's Edition pp. 104–107

Lesson 5

Sentence Diagramming

More Practice 2

C. Complex Sentences (continued)

Adverb Clause Because the rubble was so close, Yuksel could barely move.

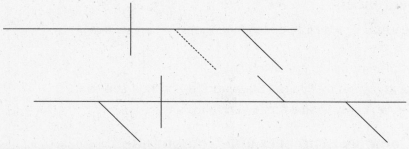

Noun Clause Used as Subject What he endured was terrifying.

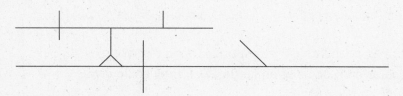

Noun Clause Used as Direct Object

Later he reported that during his long entombment he meditated, thought, and prayed.

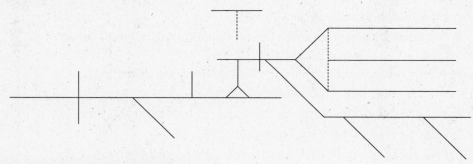

D. Compound-Complex Sentences

Finally, after someone heard his cries, a rescue team freed Er, and hundreds of his neighbors cheered.

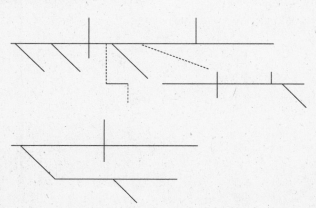

CHAPTER 4

Sentence Diagramming

Application

On a separate piece of paper, diagram each of these sentences.

A. Diagramming Simple Sentences, Compound Sentences, and Complex Sentences

1. The surface of the earth is broken into plates, and their shifting causes earthquakes.
2. Fractures between different plates are called faults.
3. The fault that is best known in the United States is the San Andreas fault.
4. California, where this fault lies, has had many earthquakes.

B. Diagramming Complex Sentences and Compound-Complex Sentences

1. Although over 40,000 earthquakes occur in a typical year, only about 40 of them cause damage.
2. How earthquakes occur has been studied by experts around the world.
3. If scientists could recognize early signs of an earthquake, they could give warnings, and many lives could be saved.
4. Some scientists have examined how the earth moves in a quake.

C. Mixed Practice

1. Do you know how a seismograph works?
2. A seismograph senses quakes with seismometers and prints a record called a seismogram.
3. Some seismometers respond if the earth moves by only one billionth of a meter, but this movement would not cause concern.
4. Plate tectonics is the theory that explains the cause of most earthquakes.
5. Subduction zones are areas where two plates collide.
6. Because great numbers of earthquakes and volcanoes occur there, the belt around the Pacific Ocean is called the Ring of Fire.
7. The size of large earthquakes is usually reported on the Richter scale, but scientists prefer the "moment magnitude" scale.
8. What scientists discover about earthquakes may save many lives.

CHAPTER 4

Sentence Fragments

Reteaching

A **sentence** is a group of words that has a subject and a verb and expresses a complete thought.

> Certain <u>events</u> in history <u>signal</u> important developments.
> **(SIMPLE SUBJECT)**　　　**(VERB)**

A **sentence fragment** is part of a sentence that is punctuated as if it were a complete sentence. Sentence fragments are incomplete thoughts because the subject or verb is missing. Punctuation errors also may result in sentence fragments. Misused phrases and clauses may result in sentence fragments. Remember, phrases and subordinate clauses cannot stand alone as sentences.

> The abbreviation a.d., the period since Christ's birth. (missing verb)
> Was the first noted historian. (missing subject)

Identifying Sentence Fragments

If a group of words is a complete sentence, write **S** in the blank. If the words form only a fragment, write **F** in the blank.

1. Invented gunpowder in Asia around 1000 A.D. _____

2. In 1215, the Magna Carta in England. _____

3. The Crusades of the 12th century encouraged trade. _____

4. Marco Polo from Venice to Asia in 1271. _____

5. Gradually brought an end to the "Dark Ages" in Europe. _____

6. The Black Death one of every ten people. _____

7. Around 1500 the Inca culture flourished in South America. _____

8. At the same time a golden age in Mexico. _____

9. The Gutenberg Bible was the first book printed in the West. _____

10. Arrived in the Americas in 1492. _____

11. Small ships braved the huge oceans. _____

12. Although they explored the coastline. _____

13. Carried by long caravans of camels across the desert. _____

14. During the Middle Ages, most people lived on farms. _____

15. After long training in the many skills required in medieval warfare. _____

16. When people were separated by mountains, deserts, and large bodies of water. _____

17. Few people received any schooling. _____

18. Because the ancient writings of Greek physicians were revered. _____

CHAPTER 5

Lesson 1

Sentence Fragments

More Practice

A. Identifying Fragments and Their Missing Parts

If the group of words is a complete sentence, write **S** on the line. If it is a fragment, write **F** and then write which part is missing: **MS** if the subject is missing, **MV** if the verb is missing, and **MB** if both the subject and verb of the independent clause are missing.

EXAMPLES The 20th century outstanding progress in science and

technology. ___*F, MV*___

Although the 20th century made outstanding progress in science

and technology. ___*F, MB*___

1. President Kennedy's interest in space exploration. _____

2. At Kitty Hawk, North Carolina, the Wright brothers flew the first plane. _____

3. The discovery of penicillin, by chance, progress in medicine. _____

4. In 1928 demonstrated the first black and white TV. _____

5. With the development of color TV. _____

6. After 1950, a growing number of women scientists. _____

7. Sandra O'Connor, the first woman appointed to the U.S. Supreme Court. _____

8. Cloned a sheep in England. _____

9. Scientists competed for the honor of discovering cures to serious illnesses. _____

10. After they contributed to research on DNA. _____

B. Correcting Sentence Fragments

Rewrite this paragraph, correcting each sentence fragment. You may add words to the fragment to make it a complete sentence, or combine the fragment with another sentence.

Tin comes from deposits of a mineral ore in rock and gravel. Mainly in Malaysia, Bolivia, and Russia. Because tin is soft and can be hammered into thin sheets, such as tin foil. It has been a useful metal since ancient times. The Egyptians used tin in ornaments and utensils. As early as 3000 B.C. Modern "tin cans" are only coated. With tin to give the cans luster. And to keep the other metal from rusting.

_____

_____

_____

For use with Pupil's Edition pp. 116–119

CHAPTER 5

Sentence Fragments

Application

A. Recognizing and Revising Sentence Fragments

Determine which of the following groups of words are complete sentences and which are fragments. After a complete sentence, add the appropriate punctuation mark and write **Correct** on the blank line. Rewrite any fragments as complete sentences, adding appropriate words and punctuation.

1. Tornadoes or rotating storms can be extremely destructive

_____

2. Faster and more violent than hurricanes

_____

3. Dark, funnel-shaped cloud around which winds spiral inward

_____

4. The diameter of a tornado can be as little as a few feet or as much as a mile

_____

5. Tornado winds 200 to 300 miles per hour

_____

6. Chiefly in the central states

_____

7. Today Doppler radar can give advance warning of tornadoes

_____

8. Still, the unpredictability of wind movement

_____

B. Rewriting Sentence Fragments

Imagine you are a recording secretary responsible for typing out the minutes of a meeting where you took sketchy notes. Rewrite the notes below, using five complete sentences.

> Call to order at 7:15 P.M. All present except Yung Hee Kim and Richard Blair. Treasurer's report, balance after payment for flyer, $925. Reeta Parakarathu to head Tornado Relief Committee to meet 9/25 in Civic Hall, 7:30 P.M. Adjournment, 8 P.M. Refreshments.

_____

_____

_____

_____

_____

CHAPTER 5

Run-on Sentences

Reteaching

A **run-on sentence** is two or more complete sentences incorrectly joined as one. A **comma splice,** or comma fault, is a run-on sentence formed when a writer incorrectly uses a comma instead of a semicolon or period. Other run-on sentences join two sentences without any punctuation.

To correct a run-on sentence, either separate the two sentences by adding the correct punctuation and capitalization, or join them correctly with a semicolon or with a comma and a conjunction.

Comma splice	Cyberspace is the information highway, you can't ignore it.
Correct divided	Cyberspace is the information highway. You can't ignore it.
Correct joined	Cyberspace is the information highway; you can't ignore it.
Correct joined	Cyberspace is the information highway, and you can't ignore it.

A. Identifying Run-on Sentences

Identify each sentence as either **Run-on** or **Correct.**

1. The Internet is a collection of computer networks, it's often shortened to "The Net." _____

2. The World Wide Web is one of the networks on the Internet. _____

3. Computers make contact with other computers on the Net by phone wires or cable, they reach out through special computers called *servers.* _____

4. The connections between servers are called *backbones,* there are also connections between different backbones. _____

5. Schools and other institutions, businesses, and individuals can place information on their servers for everyone's use. _____

6. Each source of information is called a *site,* as you surf, you click on different sites. _____

7. The Internet offers a wide variety of data, from the weather to the latest world news, it also provides entertainment, art, and shopping opportunities. _____

B. Correcting Run-on Sentences

Correct the following run-on sentences by using correct capitalization and punctuation. Rewrite the corrected sentence on the line.

1. Every Web user has an address the address has two parts. _____

_____

2. The first part is your screen name you choose the name yourself. _____

_____

3. What name would you choose, many people make up funny ones, like daffy3 _____

_____

For use with Pupil's Edition pp. 120–121

Lesson 2

Run-on Sentences

More Practice

A. Recognizing and Correcting Run-on Sentences

Correct any run-on sentence below either by separating it into two sentences or by adding the necessary punctuation and/or conjunction, such as *and, but,* and *or.* If the sentence is correct, write **Correct.**

1. The Internet is a little over 30 years old, it was created in 1967 for government

   communication. _____

   _____

2. In 1980, other computer networks were connected with the government's system, this

   provided a tremendous amount of data to anyone with a computer. _____

   _____

3. Today, over 60 million people tap into the Internet; the most popular network is the World

   Wide Web (WWW). _____

   _____

4. Since 1993 software browsers, beginning with Mosaic, dramatically increased Net usage.

   _____

   _____

B. Correcting Sentence Run-ons

Rewrite the paragraph below, correcting any run-on sentences.

   Have you ever visited the Internet, it is a fascinating experience, you can research topics for a school project, you can just go "window shopping." Many young people have set up their own Web sites Jerry is an example. He has an account with a service provider, his provider gives him three megabytes of storage for his files, Jerry started a site about his favorite sports teams.

_____

_____

_____

_____

_____

_____

_____

CHAPTER 5

Lesson 2

Run-on Sentences

Application

A. Rewriting to Eliminate Run-on Sentences

Rewrite the following paragraph to eliminate run-on sentences. Use correct punctuation, capitalization, and appropriate conjunctions as needed.

> The most popular feature of the Internet is e-mail, it allows you to exchange messages electronically with people anywhere in the world. It is fast, it is efficient, it is inexpensive. Knowing good "Netiquette" keeps you from embarrassing yourself or offending others, you can have fun using emoticons and creative abbreviations which enliven your e-mail, they also reveal some of your personality. But you also need to be careful, e-mail isn't completely private.

_____

_____

_____

_____

_____

_____

_____

_____

_____

_____

B. Correcting Sentence Fragments and Run-ons

Rewrite the paragraph on a separate piece of paper, correcting all sentence fragments and run-on sentences.

> To be connected is a basic drive of every human being, the cave dwellers of prehistoric times drew on the walls of their dwellings. To share their common goals. Ancient Egyptians wrote in pictures on their tombs. As early as 3000 B.C. Excavations in the Mideast today bring to light ancient shards. Imprinted with wedge-shaped impressions. In old Babylon, laws were written on tall stones and set in the public square. The Phoenicians created the first phonetic alphabet, the Romans expressed their protests in graffiti. About 1000 A.D. The Chinese invented movable type. The West was flooded with books. After the invention of the printing press. In the 20th century, radio, telegraph. Telephone, and TV greatly extended communication. The Internet is the final contribution of the 20th century, it has shrunk the world. And created a source of awesome information power.

For use with Pupil's Edition pp. 120–121

Lesson 1

The Principal Parts of a Verb

Reteaching

Every verb has four principal parts: **the present, the present participle, the past, and the past participle.** With helping verbs, these four parts make all the verb's tenses and forms.

The past and past participle of a regular verb are formed by adding *–ed* or *–d* to the present. Spelling changes are needed in some words, for example, *carry—carried.*

I **paint** houses. (Present)   I am **painting** a bungalow. (Present participle)
I **painted** yesterday. (Past)   I have **painted** two walls. (Past participle)

The parts of an **irregular verb** are formed in a variety of ways. Here are some examples:

Common Irregular Verbs	Present	Past	Past Participle
Group 1 Forms of the Present, Past, & Past Participle are same	cost hit hurt let put	cost hit hurt let put	(has) cost (has) hit (has) hurt (has) let (has) put
Group 2 Forms of Past & Past Participle are same	bring catch get lead sit	brought caught got led sat	(has) brought (has) caught (has) got (has) led (has) sat
Group 3 Vowel changes from *i* to *a* to *u*	begin drink ring sing swim	began drank rang sang swam	(has) begun (has) drunk (has) rung (has) sung (has) swum

Common Irregular Verbs	Present	Past	Past Participle
Group 4 Past Participle formed by adding *-n* or *-en* to the Present	do eat go grow know run see take	did ate went grew knew ran saw took	(have) done (have) eaten (have) gone (have) grown (have) known (have) run (have) seen (have) taken
Group 5 Past Participle formed from Past adding *-n* or *-en*	break lie speak steal wear	broke lay spoke stole wore	(have) broken (have) lain (have) spoken (have) stolen (have) worn

Using Correct Forms of Regular and Irregular Verbs

Complete each sentence by adding the appropriate form of the verb given in parentheses. On the line at the right, write **R** or **I** to indicate whether the verb is regular or irregular.

1. Marco Polo _____ the Europeans many innovative ideas from China. (bring) _____

2. Ann is _____ sunflowers now; last year she _____ daisies. (grow) _____

3. Laney finally _____ the lens cover back on her camera. (put) _____

4. Our kitten just _____ a fragile vase on the windowsill. (break) _____

5. The projection TV would have _____ more than we could afford. (cost) _____

6. Ken is _____ to answer the riddle that I _____ to guess earlier. (try) _____

CHAPTER 6

Lesson 1

The Principal Parts of a Verb

More Practice

A. Writing the Correct Forms of Verbs

Decide which form of each verb given in parentheses is needed: the present participle, the past, or the past participle. Write the correct form on the line.

EXAMPLE The thieves have (steal) our sandwiches. *stolen*

1. Who has (lead) the discussion at previous meetings? _____

2. Last year my friends (bring) a comedy album to my birthday party. _____

3. Ellen has just (break) her sunglasses again. _____

4. The bell for assembly has already (rung). _____

5. What kind of juice are you (drink)? _____

6. Luis soon (earn) an increase in pay. _____

7. Has the dog (sit) there all morning? _____

8. My brother has (grow) two inches this summer. _____

9. Has the photo lab (develop) the film? _____

10. Donna has (take) courses in business, math, and accounting. _____

B. Using the Correct Forms of Verbs

Underline the correct verb form of the two in parentheses. Write whether the part of the verb is the present participle, the past, or the past participle.

EXAMPLE My sister has (drank, <u>drunk</u>) the last of the milk. *past participle*

1. They have (brought, brung) me a reward. _____

2. The Senator has (spoke, spoken) to the committee about the budget. _____

3. Wilma (wore, worn) her new ski boots at the lodge. _____

4. So far this season the first baseman is (hit, hitting) at a record pace. _____

5. Troy (drank, drunk) five glasses of cider after the softball game. _____

6. Disloyalty has (cost, costed) him a valued friend. _____

7. We were (sat, sitting) in the shade. _____

8. Vanessa has (swum, swam) across the lake to the cottage. _____

9. Felice and I (sung, sang) in the choir last year. _____

10. The wedding music had already (began, begun) when the bride arrived. _____

For use with Pupil's Edition pp. 130–133

CHAPTER 6

The Principal Parts of a Verb

Application

A. Proofreading for the Correct Forms of Verbs

Draw a line through each incorrect verb form in this paragraph. Draw this proofreading symbol ∧ next to the error and, in the spaces between lines of type, write the correct form of the verb.

EXAMPLE. Have you ~~saw~~ *seen* the Falls?

    Niagara Falls, one of the wonders of the world, has became one of the world's favorite tourist attractions. For years visitors have enjoyed the magnificent view and have feeled the vibration of the tons of water roaring over the edge. When the sun shines through the mist, spectators have catched a glimpse of ethereal rainbows poised in the air. Photographers have tryed to capture all the sights on film. Hardy souls have weared plastic raincoats on walking tours to the base of the Falls, where they have experience the water thundering above them. On the boat excursion, people have knew what it's like to be surrounded by the pounding white water inside the horseshoe of the waterfall. Though little children, perhaps, were thrilled that they had swam in the motel pool, older travelers have always appreciated the awe-inspiring vision of Niagara Falls.

B. Using Verb Forms Correctly

Write a paragraph that uses at least five of these verbs and verb phrases. Underline each of the verbs and verb phrases. Make sure all verb forms are used correctly.

hid	would have stopped	was/were looking	called
swam	had been told	has/have begun	spoke
put	has/have broken	is/are going	has/have rung

_____

_____

_____

_____

_____

_____

_____

Lesson 2

Forming Verb Tenses

Reteaching

A **tense** is a verb form that shows the time of an action or a condition. Here are the most frequently used tenses.

Simple Tenses
Present (I talk)
Past (I talked)
Future (I will talk)
Present Progressive (I am talking)

Past Progressive (I was talking)
Future Progressive (I will be talking)

Perfect Tenses
Present Perfect (I have talked)
Past Perfect (I had talked)
Future Perfect (I will have talked)
Present Perfect Progressive (I have been talking)
Past Perfect Progressive (I had been talking)
Future Perfect Progressive (I will have been talking)

To **conjugate** a verb means to show its tenses in terms of person and number. Below, the present tense of talk is conjugated.

	Number	
Person	**Singular**	**Plural**
First person	I talk	we talk
Second person	you talk	you talk
Third person	he / she / it talks	they talk

A. Identifying Verb Tenses

Underline the verb in each sentence. On the blank, write the tense of the verb.

1. From the airplane window, they saw the sunset. _____

2. Mr. Eliot will be visiting Italy next summer. _____

3. Kira had designed a perfect logo for the school newspaper. _____

4. Woodchucks hibernate during the winter months. _____

5. The firefighters have extinguished the trashcan fire. _____

6. By Monday, Barry will have been working at the shoe store
for two years. _____

7. Earlier, archaeologists had been removing artifacts from the site. _____

8. Abdulla was waiting for an important message. _____

B. Forming Verb Tenses

Underline the form of the verb that correctly completes the sentence.

1. For generations, fans (have been escaping, escape) from everyday life by reading or watching science fiction.

2. If you pick up a science fiction novel, it's likely that you (had been reading, will be reading) about life on other worlds and future technology, like robots and spaceships.

3. From space travel and submarines to cordless communication and laser tools, engineers (have changed, will be changing) authors' wild ideas into reality.

For use with Pupil's Edition pp. 134–136

CHAPTER 6

Forming Verb Tenses

More Practice

A. Using Verb Tenses

Complete each sentence by writing the form of the verb indicated in parentheses.

1. (past of *seem*) The music_____ to be coming from the next floor.

2. (past progressive of *ski*) We _____ just last weekend.

3. (present perfect progressive of *score*) Rodney _____ most of our goals.

4. (future perfect of *sell*) We hope we _____ our house by next summer.

5. (future progressive of *surf*) I _____ at the north beach this afternoon.

6. (present of *cook*) Dad always _____ our dinner on Wednesday.

7. (past perfect of *be*) Sandy _____ the best tennis player.

8. (present progressive of *take*) The calf-roping contestant _____ a big chance.

B. Revising Verb Tenses

On the short line after each sentence, identify the tense of the verb. Then rewrite the sentence using a different tense. In parentheses after the sentence, identify which tense you used.

> **EXAMPLE** The neighbors were discussing rumors. *Past Progressive*
> *The neighbors had been discussing rumors. (Past Perfect Progressive)*

1. For many people, sports contribute to the formation of good character. _____

_____

2. During each game, players will be relying on each other for effective teamwork. _____

_____

3. With faithful practice, Rachel is proving her dedication to her sport. _____

_____

4. Malcolm was learning the technique of focusing on his goals. _____

_____

CHAPTER

Forming Verb Tenses

Application

A. Using Verb Tenses

Choose a favorite hobby or activity. Write a sentence about that topic using each of the following verbs. Use the verb tense indicated in parentheses.

1. make (future) _____

_____

2. learn (present perfect) _____

_____

3. change (past progressive) _____

_____

4. find (future perfect) _____

_____

5. hope (past perfect) _____

_____

6. write (present progressive) _____

_____

B. Using Progressive Verb Forms

Below are notes for an article on the city of tomorrow. Write a paragraph based on the notes. Change at least three of the verbs to the future progressive form.

> people live in a controlled climate . . . fans enjoy favorite sports out-of-doors all year long . . . robots cooking food and cleaning homes . . . most people shop by television and Internet . . . decline of physical illnesses . . . people living in safer but very controlled environments

_____

_____

_____

_____

_____

_____

_____

For use with Pupil's Edition pp. 134–136

Lesson 3

Using Verb Tenses

Reteaching

Using verb tenses correctly enables you to show the time of a single event and time relationships between different events.

These tenses show actions or conditions that are continuously true; were completed in the past; or that will occur in the future.		Present perfect shows action that began in the past and continues; past perfect and future perfect show action that occurs before another action in that time.	
Present	falls	**Present perfect**	has fallen
Past	fell	**Past perfect**	had fallen
Future	will fall	**Future perfect**	will have fallen
These tenses show action in progress at a given time.		These tenses show action that begins and is in progress before another action occurs in that time.	
Present progressive	is falling	**Present perfect progressive**	has been falling
Past progressive	was falling	**Past perfect progressive**	had been falling
Future progressive	will be falling	**Future perfect progressive**	will have been falling

A. Using Verb Tenses

Underline the verb form in parentheses that correctly completes each sentence.

1. After a career in sailing, Captain Smith (has been making, was making) one final voyage before retirement; unfortunately his final voyage was on the *Titanic.*

2. Soon after Eric (was taking, had taken) the wheel on his first day of Driver's Education, he drove over a curb.

3. As I wash the glass shelf from the refrigerator, I (am taking, will have taken) great care because I don't want it to—Oops!

4. The team might have won the football game if the receiver (had been gripping, is gripping) the ball tightly.

5. After his meeting with a skunk, our dog (has been enduring, will be enduring) a cleansing tomato-juice bath in a few moments.

6. Greg (has been tripping, tripped) when he tried to outrun his greyhound.

B. Choosing the Correct Verb Tenses

Underline the verb form in parentheses that correctly completes each sentence.

1. Watch out! On that slippery floor, it's likely that you (will fall, will have fallen).

2. As of this minute, the rain (fell, has been falling) for 26 hours straight.

3. There is a saying that the rain (falls, fell) on both the just and the unjust.

4. After he jumps from the plane, the parachutist (had been falling, will have been falling) for almost 30 seconds when his chute opens.

5. Before the snow flies, prices on winter clothes (will have been falling, will have fallen) noticeably.

6. During my first visit to an ice rink, I (was falling, had fallen) most of the evening.

7. The rain (was falling, had been falling) all day when cracks appeared in the dam.

8. The price of the company's stock (had fallen, will have fallen) to half its value before company officers admitted their mistake.

Lesson 3 **Using Verb Tenses** *More Practice*

A. Using Verb Tenses

Underline the verb form in parentheses that correctly completes each sentence.

1. Before his parents decided on a vacation with relatives in Ohio, Tim (has been hoping, had been hoping) to go to Florida.

2. Tim frowned all the time he (was packing, has been packing) his bag.

3. Before the family returns home, Tim (will have changed, changed) his attitude.

4. At the airport, his aunt greeted the family by saying, "We (will have been attending, will attend) a ball game tonight."

5. After they (had been eating, had eaten) lunch, the family visited the natural history museum.

6. The museum (had been displaying, had displayed) a dinosaur exhibit for several months when Tim saw the fossil skeleton.

7. "When the museum closes, Tim, you (will have been staring, will be staring) at those bones for more than an hour!" his mother exclaimed.

B. Correcting Verb Tenses

Each underlined verb is in an incorrect tense. Write the correct form of the verb on the blank.

1. Ever since I can remember, Grandma <u>will be making</u> her meatloaf with poultry seasoning. _____

2. Before the weather turned cooler, we <u>will spend</u> the day in the pool. _____

3. Now Lee <u>had been driving</u> his car to Mars, Pennsylvania; but next week, he will leave for Texarkana, Texas. _____

4. By the time you turn 15 years of age, you <u>were living</u> almost 5,500 days. _____

5. As Kyle steps into Jean's home, his eyes <u>had been beginning</u> to water; and he realizes she must have a cat. _____

6. Unless you keep your camp food tightly sealed, you <u>were returning</u> to find that a bear has eaten all your supplies. _____

7. The marching band <u>has been practicing</u> for an hour when the storm blew in. _____

8. Since Dr. Jackson left to provide medical services for the poor overseas, her patients <u>came</u> to her partner, Dr. Reynolds. _____

9. The aliens <u>will be flying</u> away before the officer finished writing their parking ticket. _____

10. My research paper is due tomorrow, but my printer <u>will have been malfunctioning</u> all weekend, so may I borrow yours? _____

Using Verb Tenses

Application

Changing Verb Tenses

The following Hmong folk tale is told primarily in the present tense, with some incorrect forms of verbs. On the lines below, rewrite the story primarily in the past tense, correcting all the verbs as needed. Use a separate piece of paper if needed. The first paragraph has been done for you.

Once, long ago, plants have the ability to talk and walk. They still talk to humans when the first man takes up farming.

This man comes upon a patch of corn plants growing in the forest. Weeds are pushing against the corn plants and steal their food and water. As he is walking past, the corn plants call out, "Please, sir, if you help us against the weeds, we will produce food for you."

So the man pulls out his knife and cuts down the weeds. After he finishes the job, he goes home and waits for the plants to keep their promise.

The corn plants happily grow larger. When their ears are still ripening, the plants visit the man. They tell him, "Sir, ever since you are saving us from the weeds, we are growing. We will soon have food for you. Will you build a barn for our ears? After the barn is ready, we come to you. By the time the barn is a day old, we are filling it with ears of corn." After they deliver their message, they go back to their field and wait.

The man, however, does not build a barn. Instead, he naps every day. He sleeps when the plants come to him a second time. The angry plants wake him up and say, "You are too lazy. You are not doing anything for us. So we do not do anything more for you. We are making food for you, but if you want it, you must come out and get it. And we never speak to you again."

Ever since then, humans have to work to grow their food. And plants no longer talk to us.

Once, long ago, plants had the ability to talk and walk. They were still talking to humans when the first man took up farming.

_____

_____

_____

_____

_____

_____

_____

_____

_____

_____

Name _____ Date _____

Lesson 4

Shifts in Tense

Reteaching

In most cases, use the same verb tense within a sentence to describe events that happen at approximately the same time.

> **Another researcher was digging while I was taking notes.** (both past progressive)

However, use two tenses in the same sentence in these situations:

Use a progressive form and a simple tense to describe an outgoing action interrupted by a single event.

> **Another researcher was digging when I joined her.** (past progressive / simple past)

When describing an event as a point of reference for another event, shift from a perfect tense to a simple tense.

> **Another researcher had dug the entire site before I arrived.** (past perfect / simple past)

A. Recognizing Errors in Verb Shift

Decide whether the shift in tense within each of these sentences is correct. (The situation must fit one of the two special cases described above.) Write **Correct** or **Incorrect**.

1. No one had deciphered Egyptian hieroglyphics before a French officer discovered the Rosetta Stone in 1799. _____

2. Napoleon was leading the French army in Egypt when an officer has been uncovering a black stone from the sand. _____

3. If you were examining the stone, you will be finding the same inscription written in three languages: hieroglyphics, Greek, and Demotic, an ancient Egyptian language. _____

4. Jean Francois Champollion had been comparing names in the Greek and Egyptian text on the stone when he identified the same sounds in the hieroglyphics. _____

5. After Champollion had unlocked the mystery, other researchers translated thousands of ancient Egyptian writings. _____

B. Using Shifts in Verb Tense Correctly

In each sentence, underline the correct verb from the pair shown in parentheses.

1. Archaeologists (have found, will find) preserved bodies in tombs, thousands of years after ancient Egyptians embalmed them.

2. Archaeologists were excavating a site in Bawiti, Egypt, when they (uncovered, are uncovering) at least 200 mummies.

3. Archaelogists had unearthed Ninevah, a capital of the Assyrian Empire, when they (found, were finding) a library containing letters and documents.

4. Howard Carter (was searching, is searching) for Tutankhamen's tomb for ten years before he discovered the entrance.

CHAPTER 6

Shifts in Tense

More Practice

A. Correcting Shifts in Tense

Rewrite each of the following sentences, changing the tense of the boldfaced verb to correct the unnecessary shift in tenses.

> **EXAMPLE** Debra will take woodworking and **makes** toys for her sister.
> *Debra will take woodworking and will make toys for her sister.*

1. Charlie likes tennis and **practiced** his backhand stroke for many hours.

_____

2. Marita will draw the still life, and I **am painting** a self-portrait.

_____

3. We will play charades now, and we **are having** a snack later.

_____

4. Matt **had been** late as usual, but Eva was prompt.

_____

5. We won the first-place trophy, and Joy **will win** an honorary medal.

_____

B. Avoiding Shifts in Tense

You are writing an article on cave paintings. As you read your first draft, you notice that four of your sentences have unnecessary shifts in tense. Find the sentences with errors in tense. On the lines below, write the numbers of the sentences with errors, and rewrite those sentences so that verb tenses are consistent.

> **(1)** Today, artists will admire cave paintings and have marveled at their beauty. **(2)** A discovery made in 1940 was met with great interest. **(3)** Young boys discovered paintings on the upper walls of a cave depicting bison and hunters. **(4)** When these paintings were first found, they had been called fakes. **(5)** Today, scientists have instruments that tested the age of objects such as paintings. **(6)** It is now agreed that the Stone Age paintings are genuine and are over 20,000 years old. **(7)** Probably the ancient artists perched on ledges as they paint.

_____

_____

_____

_____

_____

_____

Lesson 4

Shifts in Tense

Application

A. Correcting Shifts in Tense

As copyeditor of a magazine on antiques, you are proofreading an article on buying antiques. You notice that four of the writer's sentences have unnecessary shifts in tense. Find the sentences with errors in tense. Draw a line through each incorrect verb, insert this proofreading symbol ∧ after the error, and write the correct form of the verb in the space above the error.

Antique collecting is not a new hobby but it will be gaining in popularity

since the 1960s. Many new collectors have written to us for advice. Usually,

the writers have had difficulty deciding which items to buy first. Today, as

always, we will have advised new antique collectors to buy items that they

consider beautiful. One new antique buyer was thinking of buying furniture

before she was talking to us. Later she happily calls us back to say she had

bought a clock instead. Remember to have fun!

B. Avoiding Shifts in Tense in Writing

Imagine that you have found an old coin. You believe it is valuable, but a coin dealer tells you it is a fake. Write a paragraph telling how you feel. Use at least four sentences that contain two verbs that use the same tense or that shift tense appropriately. Draft your paragraph on a separate sheet of paper, and write the final version on the lines below.

_____

_____

_____

_____

_____

_____

_____

_____

_____

_____

_____

_____

_____

For use with Pupil's Edition pp. 142–143

CHAPTER 6

Lesson 5

Active and Passive Voice

Reteaching

When a verb's subject performs the action expressed by the verb, the verb is in the **active voice.**

My family **bought** a new home. (The subject *family* performs the action.)

When a verb's subject receives the action expressed by the verb, the verb is in the **passive voice.**

Homes **are being sold** by the builder. (The subject *homes* receives the action.)

If you wish to emphasize the receiver of the action, or if the performer of the action is not known, use the passive voice. Otherwise, use the active voice whenever possible.

To change a verb in passive voice to active voice, follow these steps: **(1)** Determine the verb and the performer of the action. In the sample sentence, the verb is *are being sold;* the performer is *builder.* **(2)** Move the performer of the action before the verb and change the verb to active voice *(builder are selling).* **(3)** Make sure the verb agrees in number with the new subject.

Revised sentence The builder is selling homes.

Identifying Active and Passive Voice

In each sentence, underline the complete verb with a single line. If the performer of the action is identified, underline that word twice. Decide whether the verb is in active voice (the subject is the performer) or passive voice (the subject is not the performer). On the line at the right, label each sentence with **A** for active voice or **P** for passive voice.

EXAMPLE a house <u>was raised</u> by the <u><u>settlers</u></u>. *P*

1. This summer the Jordan family took a camping trip. _____

2. Three weeks were spent by the Jordans in Yellowstone National Park. _____

3. They didn't borrow a friend's trailer for their trip. _____

4. Instead, they purchased a new tent. _____

5. The Jordans considered the tent their temporary home. _____

6. At the store, several different kinds of tents were examined by the family. _____

7. A small A-frame tent is assembled easily by campers. _____

8. However, with three children, the Jordans wanted a bigger tent. _____

9. The wall tent with vertical walls and an A-frame roof was chosen. _____

10. At the campground, a suitable spot for the tent was found by Mr. Jordan. _____

11. The family discovered the difficulties in pitching a tent. _____

12. The tent stakes were hammered into the ground by the teenage sons. _____

CHAPTER 6

Active and Passive Voice

More Practice

A. Identifying Active and Passive Voice Verbs

Underline the complete verb in each of the following sentences. On the line
at the right, label the verbs in active voice **A** and the verbs in passive voice **P**.

1. Masai, a people of East Africa, live in kraals, or villages. _____

2. The village is surrounded by a thick round fence. _____

3. The kraal contains about ten to twenty small huts. _____

4. The huts are constructed by the Masai of branches, mud, and cow manure. _____

5. A hole in the roof lets smoke out and light in. _____

6. The homes of the Masai are built by the women. _____

7. Young warriors, their mothers, and their sisters live in one kraal. _____

8. The elders' kraal is occupied by married men and their families. _____

B. Changing Passive Voice Verbs to Active Voice

Choose three sentences in Exercise A that use the passive voice. Rewrite them
using the active voice.

1. _____

2. _____

3. _____

C. Using Active and Passive Voice Verbs

Complete each of sentences 1 to 6 by adding a verb in the voice given in parentheses.
For sentences 7 and 8, choose the voice that makes more sense.

1. Ricardo and Angela _____ several pieces of furniture for
their first home. (active)

2. All these pots and pans _____ by my sisters at a garage
sale. (passive)

3. After dark, homeless persons _____ rides to a shelter by
search-van drivers (passive)

4. The moving company _____ my furniture into their truck.
(active)

5. All of these old clothes _____ in my grandmother's attic by
my parents. (passive)

6. In your home, who _____ the windows when they're dirty?
(active)

7. The house _____ a dark shade of blue by the painters.

8. The real estate agent _____ the house in the local
newspaper.

For use with Pupil's Edition pp. 144–145

Lesson 5

Active and Passive Voice

Application

A. Revising to Avoid Passive Voice

This paragraph uses too many passive voice verbs. Underline the verbs in passive voice and determine which of them could be changed to active voice to improve the paragraph. Then rewrite the paragraph, revising the sentences you chose.

> Adobe houses are built by people in hot, dry, desert regions. In Spanish, adobe means sun-dried bricks. Adobe is made by mixing sandy clay with water and some straw and grass. The mixture is formed into bricks by the workers. Wooden brick forms are filled with the mixture. When the bricks are dry, they are removed from the forms. Then they are placed by the workers in the sun. The bricks are baked in the sun for about two weeks. Adobe houses are lived in by people across the southwestern United States and Mexico. Adobe keeps houses in hot regions cool.

_____

_____

_____

_____

_____

_____

_____

B. Using Active and Passive Voice

How would you improve the house, apartment, or other place you live in? Write a paragraph describing the first thing you would do if you had the time, money, and skills to undertake the renovation. Use at least two verbs in active voice and at least two verbs in passive voice. Make sure that the sentences with passive-voice verbs are not weak and would not sound better with active-voice verbs.

_____

_____

_____

_____

_____

_____

_____

_____

CHAPTER 6

Lesson 6

The Mood of a Verb

Reteaching

The **mood** of a verb conveys the status of the action or condition it describes. Verbs have three moods.

Indicative mood is used to make statements and ask questions.

> **Statement** Legends are often based on real events.
> **Question**   Was Robin Hood a real person?

Imperative mood is used to make a request or give a command. Usually the subject, *you,* is understood and not stated.

> **Command** Please tell me the truth.

Subjunctive mood is used in two situations. It may be used to express a wish or state a condition that is contrary to fact. In such an expression, use *were* instead of *was.*

> I wish this story <u>were</u> true.

Also, the subjunctive mood is used for commands and requests. In these expressions, the verb must be in the base form.

> The children asked that story hour <u>be held</u> every day.

A. Identifying the Mood of a Verb

Indicate the mood of each underlined verb by labeling it with **IND** for indicative, **IMP** for imperative, or **SUBJ** for subjunctive.

1. In Greek mythology Daphne <u>was</u> a hunter.   _____

2. She wished she <u>were</u> like Artemis, goddess of the hunt, who refused to marry. _____

3. "<u>Let</u> me remain unmarried," she asked her father, Peneus.   _____

4. The god of love, Eros, <u>shot</u> the god Apollo with a golden arrow.   _____

5. This made Apollo act as if he <u>were</u> in love with Daphne.   _____

6. "<u>Leave</u> me alone," Daphne begged Apollo.   _____

7. But Apollo <u>chased</u> her through the woods.   _____

B. Using Subjunctive Mood

Underline the correct form of each verb in parentheses

1. According to a legend, the tyrant Gessler ordered that every person (bow, bows) down to his hat.

2. The townspeople wished a hero (was, were) able to defy the ruler.

3. If a champion (was, were) around to lead them, they would support him.

4. William Tell acted as if Gessler's hat (was, were) not important.

5. Gessler demanded that Tell (shoot, shoots, shot) an apple off the head of his son.

For use with Pupil's Edition pp. 146–147

CHAPTER 6

Lesson 6

The Mood of a Verb

More Practice

A. Identifying Types of Subject Complements

Identify the mood of the underlined verb in each numbered item. On the corresponding line below, write **Indicative, Imperative,** or **Subjunctive.**

(1) Legends <u>are</u> a mixture of fact and fiction. (2) According to legend, King Arthur <u>was</u> a sixth century British king. (3) No one can agree if a real Arthur existed. <u>Believe</u> in him if you like. (4) Historians wish more evidence <u>were</u> available about his life. (5) If he <u>were</u> real, he must have been a dynamic character. (6) <u>Remember</u> that the Arthurian legends are over 1,000 years old. (7) <u>Think</u> of the stories you have heard about Arthur. (8) There are some early references to King Arthur but the familiar stories about him <u>were introduced</u> hundreds of years later. (9) Stories <u>developed</u> about him and his Knights of the Round Table searching for the Holy Grail. (10) Another story concerns Excalibur. Its magic required that only the future king <u>remove</u> it from the rock.

1. _____   6. _____

2. _____   7. _____

3. _____   8. _____

4. _____   9. _____

5. _____   10. _____

B. Using the Correct Mood of a Verb

Underline the correct form of the verb. On the line at the right, indicate which mood you used. Write **IND** for indicative, **IMP** for imperative, or **SUBJ** for subjunctive mood

1. "(Tell, Tells) us the story about the king and the gold," called the students. _____

2. Because King Midas (was, were) gracious to one of his followers, Dionysus, the god of wine, rewarded him by granting one wish. _____

3. The king wished that he (be, were) able to turn objects into gold with the touch of his hand. _____

4. At first King Midas (was, were) able to enjoy his new gift, but his food and drinks turned to gold as well. _____

5. He wished that things (was, were) the way they had been before. _____

6. He turned to Dionysus for assistance. "(Help, Helps) me, please!" _____

7. The cure required that he (bathe, bathes) in the Pactolus River. _____

8. Everyone tried to imagine that he or she (was, were) hearing the story for the first time. _____

CHAPTER 6

The Mood of a Verb

Application

A. Proofreading for Correct Mood

The following passage is a manuscript for a play version of "Little Red Riding Hood."
Find six verbs that are expressed in the wrong mood for the sense of the passage.
Draw a line through each incorrect word. Then draw this proofreading symbol ∧ next
to the word and write the correction above the error. If you like, mark two additional
sentences that are not wrong but would sound better in a different mood.

Narrator, standing alone at one side of the stage, speaking to audience:

Hello! Have you come for a story? If I was you, I'd certainly expect to find a

story here. And you're in luck, because here comes a story right now.

[Little Red Riding Hood enters from one side of the stage, and the Wolf

enters from the other. Both of them ignore the Narrator, as if he was not there.]

Wolf: Greetings, little girl! What bring you into the woods today?

Little Red, speaking to the audience: My mother recommended that I am

rude to anyone I meet in the woods, and that I not answer. But it seems to

me that this wolf is friendly. I request that you tell me what to do—stop and

talk, or go on.

Narrator: All the people in the audience really must speak up. They must

answer more loudly. . . . Yes, that be better.

Wolf: Little girl, I beg that you are willing to talk. Ignore what those people

say. What do they know about me? We've never even met!

B. Using the Correct Mood in Play-Writing

Write more of the play of "Little Red Riding Hood." You may continue with the
scene begun above, or jump to a later scene. In your writing, be sure to indicate
who is talking, as in the passage above. Also, include in your passage at least two
verbs in the indicative mood, at least two in the imperative mood, and at least two
in the subjunctive mood.

_____

_____

_____

_____

_____

_____

For use with Pupil's Edition pp. 146–147

Commonly Confused Verbs   *Reteaching*

Some pairs of verbs are often used incorrectly. Do not use one when your meaning requires the other.

lie/lay *Lie* means "to rest in a flat position." (Its principal parts are *lie, lying, lay, lain.*)

> You may <u>lie</u> on that mat for a brief rest. I <u>lay</u> there before. Others <u>have lain</u> there, too, but nobody <u>is lying</u> on it at the moment.

Lay means "to place." (Its principal parts are *lay, laying, laid.*)

> You may <u>lay</u> your books on the same table where Gloria <u>is laying</u> hers. I <u>laid</u> mine there when I came in. Others <u>have laid</u> their things on it, too.

learn/teach Use *learn* when a person receives information and *teach* when a person gives information to another.

> Vincent <u>learned</u> how to do a back flip. Now he <u>teaches</u> others how to do it.

raise/rise Use *raise* when someone or something is lifting someone or something else up. (The principal parts of *raise* are *raise, raising, raised, raised.*) Use *rise* when something is lifting itself up. (The principal parts of *rise* are *rise, rising, rose, risen.*)

> <u>Raise</u> your hand for permission before you <u>rise</u>.
> When the flag-bearer <u>raised</u> the flag, we all <u>rose</u> to sing the national anthem.

set/sit *Set* means "to place something." It requires a direct object.

> <u>Set</u> your model in a safe place before you <u>sit</u>.

Using Confused Verbs Correctly

Underline the verb that correctly completes the sentence.

1. Several obstacles (lay, laid) in the path of the athlete's success.
2. Scores on the weekly quizzes have (raised, risen) three weeks in a row.
3. Yesterday the class (taught, learned) how to use the library computer.
4. On which chair will you (sit, set) at the table?
5. Our football team's success this year has (raised, risen) school morale.
6. I (lay, laid) my book bag on that desk only moments ago.
7. Do you think we have (sat, set) our goals too low?
8. Hasn't anyone ever (learned, taught) those students to cheer for a guest team?
9. When the band members finished playing, they (lay, laid) down their instruments.
10. Mrs. Noe, the math teacher, tried to (teach, learn) me the algebraic formula.
11. The curtain (raised, rose) and the show began.
12. The speaker (raised, rose) some important issues.
13. Where have you (sat, set) down your lunch trays?
14. Surely we can (learn, teach) some Spanish by listening to tapes.
15. The gym equipment (lay, laid) outside all night in the rain.
16. John (sat, set) down and started to complain.

Name ______________________ Date __________

Lesson 7

Commonly Confused Verbs

More Practice

A. Correcting Confused Verbs

Examine the boldfaced verb in each of the following sentences. If the verb is not correct, write the proper verb on the line. If the verb is correct, write **Correct.**

1. **Set** right where you are until the picture has been taken. __________
2. In gym the students **learned** the exchange student how to play football. __________
3. The dough **had** not **raised** because we forgot to add the yeast. __________
4. Yolanda **laid** in the nurse's office yesterday when she felt ill. __________
5. The fundraising campaign **is raising** money to buy new computers. __________
6. The Spirit Committee **has sit** up the chairs and tables for the dance. __________
7. The students **laid** their pencils on the desks when the test time was over. __________
8. Those freshmen **are teaching** their way around the high school. __________
9. Kiley **lies** on the floor in order for her partner to practice CPR. __________
10. Minh scores the winning goal and his teammates **rise** him onto their shoulders. __________

B. Proofreading for Confused Verbs

Five of the following sentences contain incorrectly used verbs. Rewrite those five sentences correctly on the lines below.

(1) Sally first tried to lay in a hammock at camp during free time one day. **(2)** She had taken a magazine outdoors and set on the grass to relax. **(3)** She rose from that position at once, though; the ground was still wet with dew. **(4)** Then she noticed an old net hammock strung between two trees.

(5) Setting her magazine on the hammock, Sally scrambled in and laid down. **(6)** The sides of the hammock instantly rose, closing over her like a bag. **(7)** The startled girl cautiously rose her head and pushed outward and down with her palms. **(8)** Then she began carefully climbing over the side. **(9)** The aging rope at one end of the hammock suddenly gave way. **(10)** "I seem to be back where I started!" Sally muttered, rising herself from the ground.

CHAPTER 6

Commonly Confused Verbs

Application

A. Correcting Confused Verbs

Your family is moving, and you decide to make a list of the last-minute things you have to do. After writing the list, you notice that you have confused the use of certain verbs. Rewrite each incorrect sentence, using the correct verb.

1. Take the *Wild Nature* magazines that are setting on the sofa back to the library.
2. Lay the masks that I made for the Chinese play in Mr. Po's cabinet.
3. Learn Jeffrey to use the school's public address system.
4. Ask Pedro if he has seen the stamp collection that is laying on the table.
5. Tell Harriet how to rise the flag at assemblies.
6. Remind Aaron to notify the custodian if the temperature in the lab raises overnight.
7. Get together with Jenny and set the club minutes straight.

_____

_____

_____

_____

_____

_____

_____

_____

B. Using Confused Verbs in Writing

Write one or two paragraphs about a course or class session that was unusual, in either a positive or a negative way. Use at least five of these verbs correctly in your writing:

   lie   lay   learn   teach   raise   rise   set   sit

_____

_____

_____

_____

_____

_____

_____

_____

Agreement in Number
Reteaching

A verb must agree with its subject in number. Number refers to whether a word is singular or plural. Singular subjects take singular verbs; plural subjects take plural verbs.

> This **horse runs** fast. (singular subject and verb)
> Few **horses run** faster. (plural subject and verb)

In a sentence with a verb phrase, the first helping verb agrees with the subject.

> Lately this **horse has** been running better than ever before.

A. Identifying Subjects and Verbs That Agree in Number

In each sentence, underline the subject and the verb. On the line following the sentence, write whether the two parts of the sentence **Agree** or **Disagree** in number.

1. At first horses were used only for hunting and war. _____

2. Now horses serves us in many other ways. _____

3. Ancient horse fossils have been excavated near the Mississippi. _____

4. The fox-sized ancient horse has developed into the heavy draft horse, the short pony, and the light saddle or riding horse. _____

5. Zebras and donkeys belongs to the horse family also. _____

6. A horse's size is measured by hands, that is, the distance on the palm between the index and the little finger. _____

7. A mature stallion stand about 18 hands at the withers, the high point on the back at the base of the neck. _____

8. Arabians make good saddle horses. _____

9. Bay refers to coats of brown ranging from reddish brown and tan to sandy. _____

10. Sorrel name the color of horses with lighter chestnut coats. _____

B. Making Subjects and Verbs Agree in Number

In each sentence, underline the verb in parentheses that agrees with the subject.

1. The term "quarter horse" (identify, identifies) a special American breed of horse.
2. Quarter horses (is, are) so named because they are the fastest horses in the quarter-mile race.
3. These horses (was, were) first bred over 200 years ago.
4. In those days, the race track (was, were) cut through dense forests and rarely ran more than a quarter-mile long.
5. In the American West of today, people (uses, use) this horse for work that requires quick starts and fast turns.
6. Young horses (are, is) known as foals.
7. Off the Virginia coast, Chincoteague Island (has, have) become noted for its annual wild pony roundup and auction.

For use with Pupil's Edition pp. 158–159

Lesson 1

Agreement in Number

More Practice

A. Making Subjects and Verbs Agree in Number

On the line following each sentence, write the present tense form of the verb that agrees with the subject.

1. Often famous men and women (become) attached to their horses. _____

2. Celebrities (make) their horses widely known by association. _____

3. My little brother (brag) about knowing the name of Napoleon Bonaparte's favorite horse. _____

4. Civil War Annals (record) that the crusty General Robert E. Lee loved his horse Traveler dearly. _____

5. Betty's grandmother (remember) when "Heigh Ho, Silver!" rang out every day in the *Lone Ranger* radio series. _____

6. In the Roy Rogers westerns, Trigger (go) everywhere with his master. _____

7. Thomas Jefferson's letters (reveal) that Mr. Jefferson named his horse after Don Quixote's horse, Rosinante. _____

8. For more than 2,000 years, Alexander the Great's horse (have) been known by its name, Bucephalus. _____

9. A Roman annal (tell) us that Emperor Caligula made his horse Incitatus a senator! _____

10. Many popular authors (write) stories about horses. _____

B. Correcting Agreement Errors

Underline the five verbs in this paragraph that do not agree with their subjects. On the lines below, write the numbers of the sentences in which you find agreement errors. After each sentence number, write the subject and the verb form that agrees with it.

(1) Palomino comes from the Spanish. (2) It means "like a dove." (3) Palomino horses possesses a dove-like color. (4) Some are brownish gray. (5) Other palominos shines golden in the sun. (6) Typically a palomino display a silvery white or ivory mane and tail. (7) It stand tall on slender legs. (8) Palominos lack one vertebra. (9) As a result, their bodies appears a little shorter than standard in the middle. (10) For this reason, they are known as "short-coupled."

_____

_____

_____

CHAPTER 7

Lesson 1

Agreement in Number

Application

A. Proofreading for Errors in Agreement

Find the verbs in this paragraph that disagree with their subjects. Rewrite the paragraph on the lines below. Correct all agreement errors, by changing either the number of the subject to agree with the verb or the number of the verb to agree with the subject.

A rodeo offers many thrills to the audience. Rodeo fans watches races, steer roping, and skillful riding. In some events, horses works against riders. In others, they work together with riders. Cowboys ride bucking broncs. A rider spurs the horse to make it buck. The horse try to throw the rider. Cowgirls takes part in barrel racing. In that event, horses carries their riders in a race around a pattern of barrels. What if a barrel fall? The accident cost the rider points.

_____

_____

_____

_____

_____

_____

_____

_____

B. Making Subjects and Verbs Agree in Writing

Choose one of the topics below and write a paragraph of at least five sentences about it. Use the present tense throughout. Make sure the subjects and verbs of all the sentences agree.

Stories or Films about Horses   What I Like about Horses
Famous Jockeys   Famous Horses
The Work Horses Do   The Ups and Downs of Horseback Riding
Kinds of Horses   The Loyalty of Horses

_____

_____

_____

_____

_____

_____

For use with Pupil's Edition pp. 158–159

CHAPTER 7

Lesson 2

Words Between Subject and Verb   *Reteaching*

The subject of a verb is never found in a prepositional phrase or an appositive
phrase. Such phrases may separate the subject from the verb. To find the subject,
look at the words before the phrase. Make sure the verb agrees with the subject.

> **Prepositional Phrases**
> This **string** <u>of multicolored beads</u> **glitters.** (singular subject and verb)
> The **beads** <u>on the string</u> **reflect** the light. (plural subject and verb)
>
> **Appositive Phrases**
> **Jewelry,** <u>bracelets, necklaces, rings, and such,</u> **has been** popular with humans from earliest
> times. (singular subject and verb)

A. Identifying Subjects and Verbs

Underline the subject and verb in each sentence. (Do not underline appositive
phrases.) On the line, identify whether the subject and verb are **singular** or **plural.**

> **EXAMPLE** The <u>necklace</u>, as well as the matching earrings, <u>is</u> silver. *singular*

1. Earth's hardest substance, the diamond, originates 75 miles under the earth. _____

2. The diamond, a stone of crystallized pure carbon, is the most prized
of gems.   _____

3. The rich diamond mines of Africa remain the world's major diamond
producers.   _____

4. Most diamonds for jewelry are tinged with yellow.   _____

5. Industrial diamonds, on the other hand, have a gray or brown appearance. _____

6. The toughness of diamonds makes them ideal for industrial use.   _____

7. Diamonds of the greatest rarity and value appear colorless or pale blue. _____

B. Making Subjects and Verbs Agree

Draw a line through any phrase that separates the subject from the verb. Underline
the verb that agrees with the subject.

1. A gem show with its hundreds of precious stones (provide, provides) an
afternoon of exquisite beauty.

2. Diamonds of every color, cut, and size (sparkle, sparkles) under neon lights.

3. Other precious gems such as brilliant rubies, lustrous pearls, luminous
sapphires, and bright emeralds (are, is) also very beautiful.

4. Korean amethysts, the world's clearest variety, (glow, glows) pure and translucent.

5. Smooth jade of milky green (are, is) set off in a ring by tiny, flashing diamonds.

6. Spectators, transfixed by the beauty of the jewels, (move, moves) about slowly,

7. Armed guards, each in a strategic position, (keep, keeps) watchful guard.

8. The show, merely a limited display of earth's generous riches, (take, takes) your
breath away.

CHAPTER 7

Words Between Subject and Verb
More Practice

A. Making Subjects and Verbs Agree

Underline the verb that agrees with the subject.

1. Many people (invest, invests) in gold or silver jewelry as a dependable asset.
2. Charles Lewis Tiffany, one of New York's silver merchants, (are, is) responsible for setting the standard of sterling silver in 1851.
3. Sterling silver in modern times (contain, contains) strictly 925 parts of silver and 75 parts of copper.
4. A simple necklace of fine silver (create, creates) an elegant accent.
5. Women with a cool skin undertone (wear, wears) silver jewelry best.
6. A woman with warm skin undertones (look, looks) good in gold jewelry.
7. Persons born in January (have, has) the garnet for their birthstone.
8. Many gems, like the moonstone (hold, holds) special meaning for some people.
9. Diamonds, an April child's birthstone, (symbolize, symbolizes) love.
10. Healing, a deep need we all share, (are, is) believed to be a power of the turquoise.

B. Correcting Agreement in Number

In each of these sentences, decide whether the verb agrees with the subject. If it does, write **Correct** on the line. If it does not, write the correct form of the verb on the line.

1. Gold, a dense, precious, bright yellow and lustrous metal, has always been sought after. _____

2. Early civilizations such as those of Egypt, Minos, Assyria, and Etruria was already creating beautiful artifacts of gold. _____

3. In the Middle Ages, alchemists with imagination was beginning the advance of chemistry by trying to make gold from base metals. _____

4. Gold, like many other elements, occur widely in small amounts in rocks. _____

5. Even today, international payments between one nation and another is made in gold. _____

6. Pure gold, without alloys, bear the carat stamp of "24." _____

7. One carat, from carob, "beans," equals 200 milligrams. _____

8. Twelve-carat golds, with their silver, paladium, or platinum alloys, consist of 50 percent gold. _____

9. The golden dome on that church between blocks of office buildings glow at dawn and sunset. _____

10. In China, the golden gabled roofs of the ancient imperial palace creates a city of gold. _____

Lesson 2

Words Between Subject and Verb   *Application*

A. Correcting Agreement in Number

Locate the subject and verb of each numbered sentence. If there is an agreement error, write the subject and the correct form of the verb on the lines below. If the subject and verb agree, write **Correct.**

(1) Jade, as well as other precious stones, have been valued for many years. Jade is usually white in its pure state. **(2)** Mineral impurities in the jade makes the stone turn bright yellow, red, or various shades of green. The most desired shade of jade is emerald green, known as "Imperial" jade. **(3)** This type of jade come from Burma. Jade is so tough that it is very difficult to carve. Steel chisels will not work. **(4)** Therefore, grit is rubbed over the surface until the jade wears away. Making a simple bowl can take two or three years. **(5)** Carved pieces of jade, estimated to be 3,500 years old, has been found in Mexico.

1. _____

2. _____

3. _____

4. _____

5. _____

B. Using Correct Subject-Verb Agreement

Choose one of the sets of sentence beginnings below and write your own ending. Use all three sentence beginnings in your chosen set in a paragraph of at least six sentences. Throughout the paragraph, underline the subject and verb of each sentence. Make sure that each verb agrees in number with its subject.

Set A   Mr. Burton, the embarrassed recipient of two gold watches
One of the watches, a recent birthday gift of his three brothers
The other, from his employer of 25 years

Set B   An earring with three diamonds
The maintenance men on the midnight shift
Two women with the other earring

_____

_____

_____

_____

_____

_____

_____

CHAPTER 7

Lesson 3

Indefinite-Pronoun Subjects

Reteaching

An **indefinite pronoun** refers to an unspecified person or thing. Some indefinite pronouns are always singular. They take singular verbs. Examples are *another, anybody, anyone, each, everyone, neither, nobody,* and *someone.*

<u>Neither</u> of the tour leaders **was** available.

Some indefinite pronouns including *both, few, several,* and *many* are always plural. They take plural verbs.

<u>Few</u> of the tourists **were** awake.

Other indefinite pronouns including *all, any, most, none,* and *some* can be singular or plural depending on how they are used. If the pronoun refers to one person or thing, it takes a singular verb. If it refers to two or more people or things, it takes a plural verb.

All of the <u>tourists</u> **were** sick. (There are many tourists.)

All of the <u>food</u> **was** examined. (The food is considered as only one quantity.)

To determine whether the pronoun takes a singular or plural verb, find the noun it refers to.

A. Identifying Indefinite Pronouns

In each sentence, underline the indefinite pronoun that appears as the subject. On the line, write **Singular** if the pronoun refers to one person or thing, or **Plural** if it refers to more than one. If the pronoun can be either singular or plural, draw two lines under the word naming the person(s) or thing(s) it refers to.

EXAMPLE <u>Most</u> of the medicine <u>bottles</u> are empty. *Plural*

<u>Most</u> of the <u>medicine</u> has been used. *Singular*

1. None of the socks match. _____

2. All of the detergent is used up. _____

3. Nobody knows all the answers. _____

4. Some of the buses occasionally run late. _____

5. Most of the noise comes from the air conditioner. _____

6. All of the shopkeepers want better lighting on the street. _____

B. Making Indefinite Pronouns and Verbs Agree

In each sentence, underline the indefinite pronoun used as the subject. Then underline the verb form in parentheses that agrees with the subject.

EXAMPLE <u>All</u> of the doctors (was, <u>were</u>) puzzled.

1. Most of the student council candidates (write, writes) their own speeches.

2. Many of the students (is, are) curious about the upcoming campaign.

3. None of the information (has, have) arrived yet.

4. Few of the students (has, have) declared their support for any candidates.

5. Most of the wall (is, are) available for notices.

Lesson 3

Indefinite-Pronoun Subjects

More Practice

A. Making Verbs Agree with Indefinite Pronoun Subjects

In each sentence, underline the indefinite pronoun used as the subject. Also underline the verb. If the verb agrees with the subject, write **Correct** in the blank. It it does not agree, write the correct verb in the blank.

1. All of the flaws in the programming have been corrected. _____

2. Each of the horses are beautifully groomed. _____

3. Both of the steaks on the grill looks ready to serve. _____

4. One of the toughest events are the high jump. _____

5. Several of the tornado victims have lost their homes. _____

6. Nobody in the class know her very well. _____

7. Either of those outfits look fine to wear to the concert. _____

8. Few of the senators approve of the bill. _____

9. Neither of them complains much about working such long hours. _____

10. Most of the delegates tries their best to attend all the meetings. _____

B. Using Verbs with Indefinite Pronoun Subjects

Write each numbered sentence on the appropriate line, using the correct present tense form of the verb.

The fire department sponsors several social events every year. **(1)** In the annual masquerade ball, each of the participants (wear) a different costume. **(2)** Inevitably some of the firefighters (appear) in their uniforms. They find dancing difficult in their stiff oilcloth coats. **(3)** Someone always (come) dressed as a clown. **(4)** And every year, at least one of the attendees (arrive) as a pirate. Many guests take the dress of some historical or cartoon character. **(5)** Most, however, only (don) an outlandish hat or face mask. It's always fun to guess who is in each costume.

1. _____

2. _____

3. _____

4. _____

5. _____

CHAPTER 7

Indefinite-Pronoun Subjects

Application

A. Checking Agreement of Verbs with Indefinite-Pronoun Subjects

Proofread this paragraph for errors in subject-verb agreement. Underscore any verb that does not agree with its subject.

The gymnastic exhibition for local schools begins with a roll on a drum. Each of the gymnasts prance to the center of the arena. All of the coaches stand nervously at the edge of the large mat. One of the gymnasts leap onto the high beam and balances on one foot. Another jump to grab the bar over the pit. Then he hangs from the bar by his knees. Several of the athletes heads for the mat and begin their floor exercises. Much of the competition are still to come. Someone with a love for gymnastics have much to enjoy here.

B. Using Verbs Correctly with Indefinite Pronouns as Subjects

Think of a topic about which you can write a paragraph in which each of these phrases appears as the subject of a sentence. You may use the phrases in any order, and may write additional sentences with different subjects as well. Write your paragraph on the lines below. Make sure each verb is in the present tense and agrees with its subject.

Each of us   Some of the grapes
Few of the patrons   Neither of them
Most of it   Many at the restaurant

_____

_____

_____

_____

_____

_____

_____

_____

_____

_____

_____

For use with Pupil's Edition pp. 162–163

CHAPTER 7

Compound Subjects

Reteaching

A **compound subject** consists of two or more parts joined by a conjunction, such as *and, or,* or *nor.* A compound subject whose parts are joined by *and* usually requires a plural verb.

That <u>book</u> *and* the <u>magazine</u> **are** both about fashion.

When the parts of a compound subject are joined by *or* or *nor,* the verb should agree with the part closest to it.

Either the color photo *or* the black-and-white <u>drawings</u> **show** jewelry you'd like.
Neither the <u>drawings</u> *nor* the <u>photo</u> **shows** anything cheap.

A. Making Verbs Agree with Compound Subjects

In each sentence, underline each part of the compound subject. Draw two lines beneath the conjunction that joins the parts, and one line under the verb in parentheses that agrees with the subject.

1. Fashion and design (has, have) always interested humans.

2. Ornaments and other artifacts from very early civilizations (indicates, indicate) concern for personal beauty.

3. Neither foreign cultures nor our own society (has, have) a monopoly on fashion.

4. Hairstyles and clothing (tells, tell) others something about ourselves.

5. Some teens and adults (is, are) very experimental with fashions.

6. Magazines or television often (dictates, dictate) the current fashions and hairstyles.

7. Body types or size (does, do) influence our choices of styles to wear.

8. Colors and fabrics also (influences, influence) our choices in fashion.

9. Neither men nor women (underestimates, underestimate) the value of fashion.

10. Some men and women (spends, spend) a great deal to keep up with fashion.

B. Correcting Errors in Agreement

If the verb in a sentence does not agree with its compound subject, write the correct present tense form of the verb on the line. If the verb does agree, write **Correct.**

1. The Singapore airport or other Asian terminals witnesses a wide variety of costumes daily. _____

2. The women and men passing through wear every imaginable kind of garb. _____

3. On any given day, a short man wearing a long beard and fur fez and tall, lanky girls in black leather miniskirts walks side by side. _____

4. Either women draped from head to toe in dark veils or a little girl in cornrows tied with bright ribbons boards the moving sidewalk. _____

5. Often either a long trenchcoat or bulky sweaters hangs over the arms of people arriving from Northern countries. _____

6. Neither area folks nor any other person from a torrid zone is without bright floral parasols that help thwart the intense tropical sunlight. _____

CHAPTER 7

Compound Subjects

More Practice

A. Using the Correct Verb with a Compound Subject

Write the correct form of the given verb. Make it agree with the compound subject.

1. Face paint and body colors of various types (be) found in various cultures. _____

2. Face paint or body colors (have) been used to identify a specific tribe and their members. _____

3. Natural vegetable dyes or finely-ground rock (provide) the colors. _____

4. Good makeup and effective lighting (help) transport the audience into the playwright's world. _____

5. A mime or clown (use) face paint to create new characters. _____

6. Face paint or unusual costumes (be) used by members of some rock groups. _____

7. Either formal clothes or casual wear (qualify) as appropriate for travel these days. _____

8. High-rise hairdos and the windblown look (be) equally visible in travelers. _____

9. Neither the mature person nor young people (dress) as formally as everyone once did in public places. _____

10. Occasionally either a single native of some country with distinctive dress or convention-goers in crisp business suits (stand) out on a plane. _____

11. The person with pink hair and the twins dressed identically (catch) the eye of fellow travelers. _____

12. Despite the freedom in dress today, neither satin bustles nor the high, fluted ruff of earlier eras (be) seen anywhere. _____

B. Correcting Errors in Agreement

Find the mistakes in the paragraph. For each sentence, write the correct present tense verb to agree with the subject. If the verb does agree, write **Correct.**

(1) Costumes, makeup, and lighting creates new worlds on stage or in films. (2) Both children and adults are transported to new places. (3) Either a play or a film remove the audience from the workaday world. (4) Together, the actors and the staff takes the audience to a different and sometimes fantastic world. (5) Neither costumes nor lighting are able to do more than the human mind can imagine on its own.

1. _____

2. _____

3. _____

4. _____

5. _____

For use with Pupil's Edition pp. 164–165

Compound Subjects   *Application*

A. Combining Sentences Using Compound Subjects

Rewrite the following paragraph, combining sentences where possible by using compound subjects. Use *and, or, nor, either/or,* or *neither/nor* to join the parts of the subject. Keep the action in the tense of the two original sentences that are joined.

> In the Middle Ages, a knight's outfit was beautiful as well as practical. His horse's gear, also, was splendid. In the *Tales of King Arthur,* we read this tale:
>
> Sir Gawain prepares to ride out to find the Green Knight. His horse Gringolet also prepares to accompany him. Sometimes fellow knights help Gawain dress. Sometimes the king himself helps him don his outfit. Sir Gawain receives the finest royal costume and gear. Gringolet also receives the finest costume and gear. Gawain wears a doublet (jacket) of fine cloth, a fur-trimmed short cape, gleaming steel leg and arm guards tied with gold knots, armored shoes and gloves, gold spurs, and a trusty sword. Gringolet is outfitted with a gleaming saddle with gold fringes and polished nails. Gawain is not afraid as he faces the challenge. Neither is Gringolet afraid.

_____

_____

_____

_____

_____

_____

_____

B. Using the Correct Verb with Compound Subjects

Imagine that it has become fashionable to dye hair in bright shades of red, blue, and purple. Write a commercial promoting a temporary dye that allows users to change colors easily. In your commercial announcement, use at least one example of each of these: a compound subject whose parts are joined by *and;* a compound subject whose parts are joined by *or* that takes a singular verb; and a compound subject whose parts are joined by *or* that takes a plural verb.

_____

_____

_____

_____

Other Problem Subjects

Reteaching

Here are some types of subjects that require special attention.

A **collective noun** refers to a group of people or things. Examples include *team, family, committee, jury, herd, class, staff,* and *majority.* When a collective noun refers to a group as a unit, it takes a singular verb. When it refers to a group acting as individuals, it takes a plural verb.

> The team **has** won its fifth straight game. (acting as one)
> The team **have** tried on their new uniforms. (acting separately)

Some nouns ending in –s appear to be plural but are really singular in meaning and therefore take a singular verb. Examples include *news, measles, mumps, civics, mathematics, physics,* and *molasses.*

> Measles **is** one of the diseases tamed by modern medicine.

Titles of works of art, literature, and music are usually treated as singular. Words and phrases that refer to weights, measures, numbers, and lengths of time are usually treated as singular.

> *Millions of Cats* **is** still a popular children's book.
> Ten cents **is** the daily fine for an overdue book.
> Three weeks **is** the usual loan period for checking out a library book.

Using Verbs That Agree with Problem Subjects

In each sentence, underline the subject and the form of the verb that agrees with it.

1. An orchestra (consists, consist) of a large group of musicians.
2. Seventy-five (is, are) the typical number of members in a symphony orchestra.
3. Over one-half of the orchestra (plays, play) stringed instruments.
4. *Romeo and Juliet* (is, are) a favorite among members of a symphony orchestra.
5. The audience loudly (expresses, express) its appreciation for a great performance.
6. News of celebrity guest conductors (travels, travel) quickly from one music lover to another.
7. My class (has, have) chartered a bus to attend a concert next week.
8. *Tales from the Vienna Woods* always (draws, draw) a good crowd.
9. Three hours (is, are) a long time to wait in line for tickets.
10. However, this crowd of music lovers (is, are) willing to wait even longer.
11. The physics of sound (guides, guide) architects who plan new music halls.
12. The newspaper staff (were, was) divided in their opinions about the election.
13. Mathematics (are, is) Olivia's favorite subject.
14. Three o'clock (are, is) a good time to meet.
15. The majority of the student body (participate, participates) in co-curricular activities.
16. (Are, is) two dollars an hour a fair wage?
17. The jury (state, states) that the woman is not guilty.
18. Claude Monet's *Water Lilies* (were, was) one of a series he painted when almost blind.

For use with Pupil's Edition pp. 166–168

Lesson 5

Other Problem Subjects

More Practice

A. Using Verbs That Agree with Problem Subjects

In each sentence, underline the verb that agrees in number with the subject.

1. *War and Peace* (is, are) by the Russian writer Tolstoy.
2. Physics (is, are) an exciting college major.
3. The jury (has, have) argued for over five hours over the case.
4. *Hard Times* (is, are) my favorite novel by Dickens.
5. The pride of lions (was, were) the photographic target of the tour group.
6. Ten dollars (is, are) too high a price for that cap.
7. The majority of the patrons (requests, request) mushrooms on their pizzas.
8. The entire Guernsey herd (sit, sits) when rain is predicted.
9. Cold molasses never (flow, flows) freely.
10. The committee (were, was) scheduled to cast their votes at four.

B. Writing Sentences

Complete each of these sentences by adding a present-tense verb as described
in the parentheses, and any other needed words.

    EXAMPLE (plural verb) Three pounds of potatoes _____ *make enough salad for us.*

1. (singular verb) Our stamp-collecting club _____

_____

2. (plural verb)   Our stamp-collecting club _____

_____

3. (plural verb)   A family of three bears _____

_____

4. (singular verb) A family of three bears _____

_____

5. (singular verb) The team in last place _____

_____

6. (plural verb)   The team in last place _____

_____

CHAPTER 7

Other Problem Subjects

Application

A. Proofreading for Subject-Verb Agreement

Proofread this paragraph for errors in subject-verb agreement. Draw a line through each incorrect verb. Then draw this proofreading symbol ∧ next to the word and write the correction above the error.

Rock and roll have become the leading form of popular music in this century. A rock group usually use huge amplifiers and dozens of speakers. Bill Haley and His Comets were the first famous rock band. Since then, a class of musicians known as heavy metal have created a loud, energetic style stressing screaming guitars. A punk rock group usually explore a fast and aggressive rock style, rebelling against the "rock establishment." In addition to evolving with regard to sound, rock has evolved visually, too. During the last 20 years, the majority of rock musicians has added making rock videos to their schedule.

B. Writing One-Sentence Summaries with Subject-Verb Agreement

You are responsible for writing capsule summaries of television episodes for a weekly TV guide. Read the program descriptions below. Write a one-sentence summary of each, using a collective noun from this list as the subject. Use present tense verbs.

class   family   jury   club   team   staff

1. **The Lawyers** Mitch and Raissa defend two teens against a suit brought by the Witcomb family, who was injured when the car of the teenagers hit their car after swerving to avoid a cyclist. The decision of the jury is that the teens are not guilty.

_____

_____

2. **The Panthers** The Panthers have a problem when their star quarterback, Alex, who is responsible for the 56-0 shutout in their latest game, loses his nerve. Team members conspire to restore Alex's morale by showering him with compliments.

_____

_____

3. *The Mike* Egged on by Bill Mionelli and other dissidents in the senior class, students on the school paper, *The Mike,* consider printing an editorial critical of the school administration. Editor Laura Tendry speaks up against the plan.

_____

_____

For use with Pupil's Edition pp. 166–168

Agreement Problems in Sentences   *Reteaching*

In some sentences, the placement of the subject and verb makes it hard to choose the right verb form.

A verb always agrees with its subject, never with a predicate nominative. A **predicate nominative** is a noun or pronoun that follows a linking verb and names or explains the subject. In these examples, the subject is underlined once; the predicate nominative is underlined twice.

> The <u>danger</u> in this area **is** careless <u>campers</u>.
> Careless <u>campers</u> **are** the <u>danger</u>.

A subject can follow a verb or come between parts of a verb phrase in the following types of sentences.

> **As questions: Does** this <u>watchtower</u> **overlook** the entire forest?
> This <u>watchtower</u> **does overlook** the entire forest.

> **Beginning with *Here* or *There*:** Here **are** the volunteer <u>firefighters</u>.
> The volunteer <u>firefighters</u> **are** here.

> **Beginning with a phrase:** Over the trees **rises** a smoky <u>plume</u>.
> A smoky <u>plume</u> **rises** over the trees.

The easy way to find the true subject of these sentences is to: (1) turn the sentence around so that the subject comes before the verb; (2) determine whether the subject is singular or plural; and (3) make sure the subject and verb agree.

Solving Agreement Problems

In each sentence, find and underline the subject. Then underline the correct verb.

1. (Is, Are) you able to imagine a trip through time to Cleveland in 1944?
2. The sound (is, are) two explosions of tanks of natural gas within 20 minutes of each other.
3. There (was, were) a leak in one of the huge tanks.
4. The results of the leak and the explosions (is, are) a disaster.
5. Surrounding the tanks (is, are) factories and many small homes.
6. Because of the intense flash of heat, there (is, are) many people killed instantly.
7. In addition to the first destruction (come, comes) many scattered explosions in the streets.
8. How (does, do) firefighters cope with vaporizing gas running into sewers and, from time to time, blowing out manhole covers?
9. Through 20 blocks of the city (spread, spreads) the vicious flames.
10. Running from place to place (is, are) people searching for family members.
11. Miraculous escapes (is, are) the most exciting topic of discussion.
12. Soon, around the burning district (is, are) shelters set up in schools and churches.
13. The cost in human lives (is, are) 130 people killed.
14. Also, there (is, are) 79 homes, 2 factories, 217 cars, 7 trailers, and 1 tractor destroyed.

Agreement Problems in Sentences

More Practice

A. Solving Agreement Problems

In each sentence, find and underline the subject. Then write the present tense form of the verb that agrees with the subject.

1. Among the earliest recorded disasters (be) the Great Fire of London in 1666 that destroyed 13,000 houses and displaced 80,000 people. _____

2. Incredibly, the number of people killed in the Great Fire (be) only six! _____

3. One benefit of the fire (be) many handsome buildings erected after the fire that are still standing. _____

4. Simultaneous with the Great Chicago Fire of 1871 (occur) the forest fires of Michigan and Wisconsin. _____

5. Out of the bone-dry forests (blaze) a raging wall of flame that engulfs the lumber town of Peshtigo, Wisconsin. _____

6. How (be) violent windstorms leashed in? _____

7. The fiery winds (be) the death of 1,200 townspeople, 900 more than the number killed in the fire of Chicago that same night. _____

8. Against the doors of a burning New York nightclub (push) hundreds of doomed patrons. _____

9. In the nightclub, filled with 1,000 people, there (be) only one revolving door and one other door, opening inward. _____

10. Why (do) the public and their city administrations wait for disasters to push them into regulating safety conditions? _____

B. Correcting Agreement Errors

Find the four sentences in this paragraph in which the verb does not agree with the subject. On the lines below, write the number of each of those sentences and the correct verb forms.

(1) How is fire prevention carried out for the public? (2) High on the list of prevention measures come inspection of public buildings and private homes. (3) Also in use are safety education of the public and arson investigations. (4) In every city there is communication systems like the telephone, fire alarm boxes, and automatic signaling devices to alert firefighters to fires or explosions. (5) Do every fire department have the main kinds of trucks— pumpers, ladder trucks, and rescue vehicles? (6) Some necessary equipment are fire resistant coats, boots, gloves, helmets, and masks.

_____

_____

_____

Agreement Problems in Sentences

Application

Revising for Sentence Variety and Agreement

The following paragraph contains sentences with unusual subject-verb placement that makes them overly dramatic. In addition, several of the sentences have errors in subject-verb agreement. Revise the paragraph to sound more natural by using normal subject-verb order in a few of the sentences. Remember to make all verbs agree with their subjects and keep verbs in the present tense.

Perhaps one of America's most devastating national disasters are the San Francisco earthquake. With a violent trembling on the morning of April 18, 1906, shakes the earth. Severely damaged are the city electric wires, gas mains, and water mains. Into flame shoots many hundreds of homes and other buildings. At a total standstill is all communication and water availability. As a result, there rages fires unchecked for three days. Gone are the lives of 3,000 people. Gone is 300,000 homes. Wiped out is 28,000 commercial buildings lying in total ruin. Here in the aftermath of one of the world's worst city conflagrations are lost $500 million. But here also from out of the tragedy rises a new city and a new hope. And, unbelievably, here, less than ten years later, proudly opens the Panama Pacific International Exposition honoring the newly launched Panama Canal.

_____

_____

_____

_____

_____

_____

_____

_____

_____

_____

_____

_____

_____

_____

Nominative and Objective Cases

Reteaching

Personal pronouns change their case depending on whether they function as subjects or as objects. Personal pronouns that function as subjects or as predicate nominatives are in the **nominative case.**

	First Person	Second Person	Third Person
Singular	I	you	he, she, it
Plural	we	you	they

Subject	<u>We</u> read several Greek myths in English class.
Predicate nominative	It was <u>we</u> who completed the project.
Part of compound subject	Darryl and <u>I</u> read the story of Orpheus and Euridice.

Personal pronouns that function as direct objects, indirect objects, or as objects of prepositions are in the **objective case.** Also use the objective case of the pronoun when it is part of a compound object construction.

	First Person	Second Person	Third Person
Singular	me	you	him, her, it
Plural	us	you	them

Direct object	Can you help <u>me</u> remember the Greek names?
Indirect object	Mr. Clark told <u>us</u> to refer to the genealogical chart.
Object of preposition	Many of the stories were new to <u>us</u>.

A. Identifying the Case of a Pronoun

Identify the case of each boldfaced personal pronoun in the following sentences. On the line write **N** for nominative or **O** for objective.

1. Orpheus could play the harp beautifully; **he** was known for his skill. _N_

2. Orpheus fell in love with the beautiful Euridice and soon married **her.** _O_

3. One day Euridice was bitten by a snake, and **she** died. _N_

4. Orpheus was lost without **her** and became determined to bring her back. _O_

5. **He** traveled to the house of Hades in the land of the dead to plead for her life. _N_

B. Identifying the Case of a Pronoun

Underline the correct pronoun to complete each sentence.

1. Hades told (they, (them)) they could both leave, but Orpheus could not look back at Euridice.

2. ((They,) Them) left together, with Euridice following Orpheus.

3. Orpheus forgot the warning, and ((he) him) looked back at Euridice, who immediately began to fade away.

4. Orpheus and (her, (she)) were separated again, this time with no hope of rescue.

5. A terrible lesson about obedience to the gods was made clear to both Orpheus and ((her,) she).

For use with Pupil's Edition pp. 181–184

Nominative and Objective Cases

More Practice

A. Using the Correct Case of Personal Pronouns

Underline the correct form from the pronouns in parentheses.

OP 1. When Atalanta was born and her father saw that she was a girl, he ordered his servants to leave (she, **her**) on the mountains to die.

S 2. Alone in the wilderness, (**she**, her) cried until a she-bear fed her.

OP 3. Atalanta grew up with hunters; she stayed with (they, **them**) until she was grown.

OP 4. When she was grown, she found her father's home and went to live with (**him**, he).

S 5. She was amazingly strong and fast because (**she**, her) had grown up under difficult circumstances.

6. Many young men wanted to marry her, but she had no time for (they, **them**).

OO 7. The legend tells (we, **us**) that Atalanta declared that she would marry no man unless he could outrun her.

S 8. If a man should fail to win the race, (**he**, him) would be put to death.

OP 9. When Milanion saw Atalanta, he fell in love with (she, **her**) despite the danger.

S 10. Atalanta and (**he**, him) began a race together, but soon he fell behind.

DO 11. Milanion, to distract Atalanta, threw a golden apple ahead of (she, **her**).

OO 12. Milanion saw Atalanta stop to pick up the apple and fall behind (he, **him**).

SC 13. Onlookers were delighted at the closeness of the race, and (**they**, them) cheered.

S 14. (**We**, Us) are not surprised that Atalanta stopped for two more golden apples tossed before her.

S 15. At last, the goddess Aphrodite made the apples feel unbearably heavy in Atalanta's pockets, and Milanion won the race. (Him, **He**) and Atalanta were soon wed.

B. Choosing Personal Pronouns

Fill in the blanks in the following sentences with the appropriate personal pronouns. Then on the lines, identify the case of each pronoun you supply.

1. The speaker urged _____ to set our goals carefully. _____

2. Have you seen the comet? I saw _____ clearly last night. _____

3. Lydia, _____ could get more for your money at outlet stores. _____

4. Mark refinished the table after Jen showed _____ how to do it. _____

5. In his autobiography _____ explained his motivations. _____

6. The queen commanded that her subjects bow down before _____. _____

7. The customers demanded that the price of admission be refunded to _____. _____

8. Clyde Barrow was a notorious criminal; both _____ and his partner, Bonnie Parker, died violent deaths. _____

Nominative and Objective Cases

Application

A. Proofreading

Proofread the following story to make sure that the correct cases of pronouns have been used. When you find a pronoun used incorrectly, cross it out. Then insert this proofreading symbol ∧ and write the correct pronoun above it.

Long ago, the god Helios was in charge of the sun. Every day, he drove the sun chariot from east to west across the sky. The job she did was difficult and dangerous. If the chariot were to get loose, they could cause incredible damage. The son of Helios, Phaethon, was sure that he could drive the sun chariot as well as his father. He tricked his father into giving he permission to drive the chariot one day. Helios tried to dissuade her, but to no avail.

On the fateful day, Phaethon climbed into the chariot. His father gave him last-minute instructions. He told Phaethon to keep a steady hand on the reins, or the horses would carry he and the sun away. Phaethon was sure we could handle the job and did not listen to his father. When the time came to depart, Phaethon took the reins, and immediately the horses knew that it was inexperienced. Them carried him away and flew straight up into the sky, then back down to the earth. They set the forests of the earth on fire and burned many people. Finally, Zeus sent a thunderbolt toward Phaethon that shot down the horses and he. The horses were saved, but Phaethon died in the fiery crash. Phaethon's sisters grieved his death, and she stood in one spot weeping for so long that their feet turned into roots, and it became poplar trees.

B. Using Pronouns in Writing

Retell a familiar folktale or myth. Be sure to use personal pronouns correctly.

_____

_____

_____

_____

_____

_____

_____

_____

_____

(For use with Pupil's Edition pp. 181–184)

The Possessive Case

Reteaching

Personal pronouns that show ownership or relationships are in the **possessive case.**

	First Person	Second Person	Third Person
Singular	my, mine	your, yours	his, her, hers, its
Plural	our, ours	your, yours	their, theirs

A possessive pronoun can be used in place of a noun. Some of these pronouns can function as a subject or an object.

> Many people have hobbies. <u>Mine</u> is stamp collecting. What is <u>yours</u>?

A possessive pronoun can be used to modify a noun or a gerund. The pronoun comes before the noun or gerund it modifies.

> <u>My</u> collecting has taught me much about the history of many countries.

Identifying Possessive Pronouns

Underline the possessive pronouns in the following sentences.

1. Many people report that their hobby is collecting just about anything.
2. For example, my hobby is collecting matchbooks.
3. Every time I go to a restaurant, I ask for one of their matchbooks.
4. My collection advertises local restaurants, restaurants in other cities, and even restaurants in other countries that my friends have visited.
5. I told Audrey about my hobby, and she explained hers.
6. Instead of collecting things, Audrey has fun making her own jewelry.
7. In our town, we have a store that specializes in beads from all over the world.
8. Audrey checks the store about twice a month to see if their stock has changed.
9. Theirs is the honor of handling special, handmade beads from a tribe in South America.
10. When Audrey learns that a new shipment has arrived, she makes it her business to visit the bead store.
11. She picks up jewelry beads for her relatives and friends to give them on their birthdays.
12. Along the way, she saves a few beads for her own collection.
13. Ken reports that his current hobby is woodworking.
14. Ken says that most rooms could use a fine wood piece; I know that ours could.
15. Our neighbor's hobby is gardening, and our whole street benefits from Mrs. Ortiz's hard work.
16. She spends every one of her spare minutes with her garden, weeding its beds and planning its layout.
17. You know about our hobbies; now what is yours?
18. Find the one thing that catches your imagination, and that will be it.

CHAPTER 8

Lesson 3

The Possessive Case

More Practice

A. Identifying Possessive Pronouns

Underline the possessive pronouns in the following sentences.

1. Have you seen my postcard collection?
2. I started collecting postcards just before my 12th birthday.
3. Other fathers join their sons in playing catch, but mine joins me in organizing my collection.
4. Some of our collection shows busy street scenes from the turn of the century.
5. We were surprised to learn that postcards first appeared around 1870, even though our oldest cards date back only to 1910.
6. We share our hobby with people all over the country who collect postcards.
7. Their collections may concentrate on historical subjects or works of art.
8. We have learned that many people enjoy collecting pictures of their favorite pets.
9. Many of my father's collection feature topics related to World War I.
10. His is an older collection; mine concentrates on more modern subjects.
11. I have a particular interest in architecture, so I look for postcards of my favorite buildings in cities around the world.
12. With some of our fellow collectors, the Titanic is a favorite topic.
13. When our friends and family go on vacation, they always send us postcards from their destinations.
14. Someday I hope my collection will be worth some money, but profit isn't my primary goal in collecting.
15. If you were a collector, what would your motivation be?

B. Using Pronouns Correctly

Fill in the blanks in the following sentences with appropriate possessive pronouns.

1. This library is known for _____ collection of historic documents.

2. I envy you your beautiful garden; I'm afraid _____ is full of weeds.

3. When _____ family gets together, our father always takes a family photo.

4. You pay for _____ selections at the cash register by the door.

5. Before visitors enter our house, they take off _____ shoes.

6. After the buyers sign the contract for the home, it is _____.

7. Your dog may be well behaved, but we love _____ for his affectionate nature.

8. I'm afraid I left _____ gloves on the bus, and now they're gone.

For use with Pupil's Edition pp. 185–189

CHAPTER 8

The Possessive Case
Application

A. Proofreading for Pronoun Errors

Proofread the following paragraph, looking for errors in possessive pronoun usage. When you find a possessive pronoun used incorrectly, cross it out. Then insert this proofreading symbol ∧ and write the correct pronoun above it.

     If you want a hobby that increases your endurance and also gets you where you want to go, try bicycling. Some bicyclists put well over a thousand miles on his bikes over the course of a single year. They have strong legs and increased aerobic capacity as a result. I took up bicycling when I was in mine early teens. I wanted to visit my friends, but my folks didn't always have time to get me around our town. With a bike, I had my freedom. After a while, I found that my pleasure came, not only from reaching their destination, but also from the cycling itself. I discovered that our town has a cycling club that meets regularly. At there meetings, members give hints for good places to cycle, and they plan there upcoming outings. Their motto is "If you can get there in a car, you can get there on you're bike." We have sponsored century rides in which the goal is to cycle 100 miles in a day. I proudly wear the T-shirt I was awarded after my first century ride. It's very presence in my closet reminds me of my victory over fatigue.

     If you are looking for a great hobby, why not spend some of his free time bicycling? Our legs and lungs will be glad you did.

B. Using Pronoun Cases Correctly in Writing

Write a paragraph about a memorable experience in your past. Use the correct cases of personal pronouns in your sentences. Be sure to use at least five pronouns in the possessive case.

_____

_____

_____

_____

_____

_____

Name _____ Date _____

Lesson 4

Using *Who* and *Whom*

Reteaching

The case of the pronoun who is determined by the function of the pronoun in the sentence. *Who* and *whom* can be used to ask questions and to introduce subordinate clauses.

Nominative	who, whoever
Objective	whom, whomever

Who is the nominative form of the pronoun. In questions, *who* is used as a subject or as a predicate pronoun. *Whom* is the objective form. In questions, *whom* is used as a direct or as an indirect object of a verb or as the object of a preposition.

Subject   In *A Tale of Two Cities,* <u>who</u> sat below the guillotine?
Object   Of all the characters, <u>whom</u> did you like best?

Use *who* when the pronoun is the subject of a subordinate clause. Use *whom* when the pronoun is an object in a subordinate clause.

Subject of clause   It was Madame Defarge <u>who</u> sat below the guillotine.
Object in clause   The character <u>whom</u> we all like best is Sydney Carton.

Using *Who* and *Whom* Correctly

Choose the correct pronoun to complete each of the following sentences.

1. (Who, Whom) is the most memorable character from literature?
2. One memorable character, at least the one (who, whom) I remember most easily, is Roderick in Edgar Allan Poe's "The Masque of the Red Death."
3. (Who, Whom) was his sister?
4. They were the people (whom, who) hosted the bizarre party in their mansion.
5. Perhaps my favorite character is Fagin, (who, whom) ran a ring of street urchins in Charles Dickens's *Oliver Twist.*
6. By (who, whom) was young Oliver finally rescued from Fagin's clutches?
7. Miss Havisham of *Great Expectations* is the old lady (who, whom) lives in the past.
8. For (who, whom) did the lonely Miss Havisham pine after he left her at the altar?
9. Some people might choose Captain Ahab, (who, whom) lost his leg to the whale Moby Dick.
10. (Who, Whom) was the narrator in the story of *Moby Dick?*
11. I have to thank (whoever, whomever) recommended that I read *To Kill a Mockingbird.*
12. In that book, I met a character (who, whom) I greatly admired—Atticus Finch.
13. Atticus was a lawyer (who, whom) was defending an African-American man (who, whom) had been unfairly accused of committing a crime.
14. (Who, Whom) else would have had enough courage to do the right thing?
15. There is a list of good books for summer reading in the library, available to (whomever, whoever) wants it.

CHAPTER 8

For use with Pupil's Edition pp. 187–189

Lesson 4

Using *Who* and *Whom*

More Practice

A. Identifying the Function of *Who* and *Whom*

In the following sentences, identify the function of *who* or *whom*. If a sentence uses *who,* underline once the verb of which it is the subject. If a sentence uses *whom,* underline twice the verb or preposition of which it is an object.

EXAMPLES   The detective discovered **who** <u>had committed</u> the series of robberies.

There is the man **whom** the authorities <u>are seeking</u>.

1. **Who** called you on the telephone?
2. **Whom** did the city council choose as the architects of the new city hall?
3. Do you remember **who** caught the touchdown pass in the final game?
4. The actor **whom** you are replacing is recovering nicely from his illness.
5. I bought the CD of the group **whom** I saw last Saturday.
6. We met an astronaut **who** had flown in the space shuttle.
7. **Who** remembers the words to this song?
8. From **whom** do I buy my ticket to the play?

B. Using *Who* and *Whom* Correctly

Choose the correct pronoun from those in parentheses in the following sentences.

1. William Shakespeare's plays provide us with characters (who, whom) touch audiences even today.
2. (Whom, Who) can forget the star-crossed lovers, Romeo and Juliet?
3. The feuding families (who, whom) kept them apart caused their deaths.
4. The character with (who, whom) I identify most is Hamlet.
5. This is a person (whom, who), like me, can never make up his mind.
6. (Who, Whom) did Hamlet's indecision and seeming madness harm the most?
7. (Who, Whom) did Macbeth kill in order to gain power?
8. Was it Macbeth or was it Lady Macbeth (whom, who) was more dangerous?
9. Julius Caesar, (whom, who) was ruler of Rome, was assassinated by his "friends."
10. In Shakespeare's play, Mark Antony is the character (who, whom) says, "I have come to bury Caesar, not to praise him."
11. In *King Lear,* Cordelia is the daughter (who, whom) her father accuses of ingratitude.
12. (Whom, Who) were Cordelia's sisters (who, whom) actually were guilty of treachery against their father?

CHAPTER 8

Using *Who* and *Whom*

Application

A. Proofreading for *Who* and *Whom*

Proofread the following paragraph. When you find the pronoun *who, whom,* or *whose* used incorrectly, cross it out. Then insert this proofreading symbol ∧ and write the correct pronoun above it.

The characters in the play *A Raisin in the Sun* by Lorraine Hansberry find themselves in conflicts among themselves and with society in general. Walter Lee Younger is a bitter and difficult young man to who life has handed a raw deal. Instead of being a financial success, he is a chauffeur who dreams of starting his own business. Ruth Younger, Walter's wife, tries hard to maintain a normal life for their son, Travis, who sleeps on the sofa in the Youngers's crowded apartment. Beneatha is Walter's sister, who Walter secretly envies because she is going to medical school. Mama is Walter's mother, whom also lives in the apartment. She is the family matriarch, who's husband died recently.

Whom should get the money that Walter's father left the family? Who's cause is most worthy? Should the money go to Beneatha, who needs it to finish school? Should it go to Walter, for who this business venture is crucial? Should Mama set aside the money for Travis, who's future is in jeopardy because of the conflict between Walter and Ruth? Or should Mama spend it on a house for whoever wants to live with her?

B. Using *Who* and *Whom* in Writing

Rewrite each sentence below, using a subordinate clause introduced by or containing *who* or *whom*. Use the pronoun given in parentheses in your new sentence.

EXAMPLE I recognize the author; she wrote this book. (who)
I recognize the author who wrote this book.

1. F. Scott Fitzgerald was a gifted American novelist; he immortalized the Jazz Age. (who)

_____

2. Francois Duvalier was a dictator of Haiti; many people feared him. (whom)

_____

3. Charles Lindbergh flew alone across the Atlantic and earned instant fame. (who)

_____

4. The identity of that person is unknown; Shakespeare wrote his sonnets to her. (whom)

_____

For use with Pupil's Edition pp. 187–189

CHAPTER 8

Pronoun-Antecedent Agreement

Reteaching

A pronoun must agree with its antecedent in number, gender, and person. An **antecedent** is the noun or pronoun that a pronoun refers to or replaces.

If the antecedent is singular, use a singular pronoun. If it is plural, use a plural pronoun. Use a plural pronoun to refer to nouns or pronouns joined by *and*. A pronoun that refers to nouns or pronouns joined by *or* or *nor* should agree with the noun or pronoun nearest to it.

> The young <u>girl</u> paints portraits. <u>Her</u> work is popular among wealthy clients.
> The <u>students</u> are apt, and <u>they</u> show amazing abilities at an early age.
> A <u>duke</u> and his <u>wife</u> commission the girl to paint <u>their</u> portraits.
> Neither her father nor her <u>sisters</u> can conceal <u>their</u> pride.

A collective noun such as *committee* may be referred to by either a singular or a plural pronoun. The number of the collective noun is determined by its meaning in the sentence. Use a singular pronoun if the collective noun names a group acting as a unit. Use a plural pronoun if the collective noun shows the members or parts of a group acting individually.

> The committee publishes <u>its</u> stands on all important issues. (singular)
> The committee cast <u>their</u> votes by secret ballot. (plural)

The **gender** of a pronoun must be the same as the gender of its antecedent. Remember that gender refers to the forms of personal pronouns—masculine (*he, his, him*), feminine (*she, her, hers*), or neuter (*it, its*). Do not use only masculine or only feminine pronouns when you mean to refer to both genders. The purpose of gender-free language is to make sure you include everyone.

> The <u>artist</u> was famous for the speed with which <u>she</u> painted.

Identifying Pronouns and Their Antecedents

In each sentence underline the pronoun once and the antecedent twice.

1. Elisabetta Sirani was a popular painter in the 1600s, although she has been nearly forgotten.
2. Elisabetta's father was a painter, and he tutored Elisabetta at a time when girls were not expected to excel in any profession.
3. When Giovanni saw that Elisabetta had talent, he began to dream of commissions.
4. The people of Bologna were impressed with their talented townsperson's work.
5. Bologna invited Elisabetta to paint a scene from the life of Christ for its church.
6. Elisabetta opened a painting school; the student body were quick to prove their talent.
7. Neither Elisabetta nor the popular painter's sisters were allowed to rest from their work for long.
8. Each painting had its own requirements and demands.
9. Elisabetta and the other daughters tried to please their father with endless toil.
10. Although Elisabetta wanted to rest, her father set unreachable goals.
11. Giovanni ignored Elisabetta's fatigue; he continually expected perfection.

Lesson 5

Pronoun-Antecedent Agreement

More Practice

A. Identifying Pronouns and Their Antecedents

In each sentence underline the pronoun once and the antecedent twice.

1. Matthew Henson longed to embark on his own adventure.
2. As an African American just after the Civil War, Henson had to deal with a prejudiced society and all its restrictions.
3. In 1887, Henson accompanied Robert Peary on his exploration of Nicaragua.
4. Peary and Henson set their next goal—to reach the North Pole.
5. To survive in the north, Henson studied the Inuit people and copied their ways.
6. Peary soon discovered that Henson and his survival skills were essential.
7. The native people taught Henson their time-tested methods of driving a dogsled.
8. Members of the expedition had their share of health problems, including frostbite.
9. Some sled dogs couldn't stand the weather; they often died without warning.
10. Henson and Peary reached their goal—reaching the North Pole—in 1909.
11. While Peary became famous, Henson and his contribution were forgotten for many years.

B. Making Pronouns and Antecedents Agree

Underline the pronoun that correctly completes each sentence. Then underline the antecedent(s) of the pronoun.

1. Two cardinals make (its, their) home in that tree every spring.
2. Juan and Louis compared (his, their) collections of rare coins.
3. Flower lovers prize the rose for (its, their) delicate scent.
4. George Bernard Shaw didn't become a successful playwright until the publication of a collection of (its, his) plays.
5. Like other gifted child performers, Shirley Temple was known for learning (her, their) lines quickly.
6. Those directors shot (his, their) films on location in Australia.
7. Katie and Abbie are both in (her, their) first year of high school.
8. That mother seal lost (her, their) pup during the ice storm.
9. Brazilians celebrate (its, their) independence day on September 7.
10. The panther is quite beautiful; (its, their) coat is jet black.
11. The team is excited about (its, their) new uniforms.
12. Neither the ticket-taker nor the ushers have any of (his, their) programs left.
13. All you students taking the test will need (their, your) identification cards.
14. The southbound flock of geese made (their, its) characteristic *V* in the fall sky.
15. Marilyn and her brother pooled (his, their) money for the party.

Lesson 5

Pronoun-Antecedent Agreement

Application

A. Making Pronouns and Antecedents Agree

Fill in the correct pronouns in the following sentences.

1. Mystery novels are admired for _____ clever plots and colorful characters.

2. Some detective fiction is also praised for _____ vivid description of setting.

3. Among the best-loved fictional detectives is Sherlock Holmes, who sometimes relied on _____ even smarter brother.

4. Miss Jane Marple, the English detective in many of Agatha Christie's novels, did much of _____ sleuthing in the countryside.

5. In mysteries, Donald J. Sobol features as _____ hero a remarkable young man named Encyclopedia Brown.

6. I love mysteries, and _____ favorite detective is Robert B. Parker's Spenser.

7. A mystery novelist's fans are likely to form a club based on _____ delight in that author's work.

8. You can join the club if you are willing to share _____ copies of Agatha Christie's mysteries.

B. Writing with Pronouns

Write a description of a recent family celebration. Be sure to include at least six personal pronouns with clear antecedents.

_____
_____
_____
_____
_____
_____
_____
_____
_____

Lesson 6: Indefinite Pronouns as Antecedents

Reteaching

A personal pronoun must agree in number with the indefinite pronoun that is its antecedent.

Indefinite Pronouns

Singular		Plural	Singular or Plural
another	neither	both	all
anybody	nobody	few	any
anyone	no one	many	most
anything	nothing	several	none
each	one		some
either	somebody		
everybody	someone		
everyone	something		
everything			

Use a singular pronoun to refer to a singular indefinite pronoun. Use a plural pronoun to refer to a plural indefinite pronoun.

Everyone had a different reason for his or her recklessness.

Many of the observers could not overcome their disbelief.

Some indefinite pronouns can be singular or plural. Use the meaning of the sentence to determine whether the indefinite pronoun is singular or plural.

Some of the water makes its way over the Canadian side of the falls.

Some of the daredevils met their deaths at Niagara Falls.

Using Indefinite Pronouns

Choose the correct pronoun from those in parentheses.

1. Most of the people who visit Niagara Falls derive (his or her, their) enjoyment by simply watching the water fall and listening to it roar.
2. A few of the visitors risk (their, his or her) lives in an attempt to conquer the Falls.
3. Anybody who goes over the Falls in a barrel should have (their, his or her) head examined.
4. Only a few of us would ever risk (his or her, our) lives in this foolish way.
5. Either of the sides—the American or the Canadian—presents (their, its) own challenges.
6. You would think that none of the people who went over it in barrels could emerge with (its, their) health intact, but some actually did.
7. In 1901, one of the hopeful daredevils, Anna Taylor, took (their, her) chances and successfully went over the Falls in a barrel.
8. Daredevils everywhere were enchanted by her successful trip; another attempted the feat in 1911, spending months recuperating from (his, their) adventure.

Indefinite Pronouns as Antecedents

More Practice

A. Identifying Indefinite Pronouns

Underline the indefinite pronoun in each sentence. Then underline the correct pronoun(s) in parentheses.

1. Several of the containers in the chemistry lab were missing (its, their) labels.
2. Everyone has paid (his or her, their) part of the rental fee.
3. Many of the musicians in the band bought (his or her, their) own instruments.
4. None of the sulfur is in (its, their) flask.
5. All of the gymnasts practiced (his or her, their) routines before the tournament.
6. Neither of the girls brought (her, their) swimsuit.
7. If anyone is interested, have (him or her, them) fill out an application.
8. Nobody wanted (his or her, their) lunch after seeing that film.
9. Both the stores raised (its, their) prices.
10. Some of the architects have already sent in (his or her, their) designs.
11. Everything was returned to (its, their) owner.
12. Most of the seasoning had lost (its, their) flavor.

B. Using Pronouns Correctly

In each sentence below, decide whether the pronouns agree with their antecedents. If the sentence is correct, write **Correct** on the line. If it contains a pronoun that does not agree with its antecedent, rewrite the sentence correctly on the line.

1. All of the squirrels were busy gathering its food for the long winter.

   _____

2. Everyone in the class quickly sat in their assigned seat.

   _____

3. Will anyone who can run a projector give the principal his or her name?

   _____

4. Each of the musicians tuned their own instrument.

   _____

5. Do all of the actors have his or her scripts handy?

   _____

6. Has anybody here lost these proofs of his yearbook photos?

   _____

7. Neither of the scientists completed their experiment on time.

   _____

Indefinite Pronouns as Antecedents

Application

A. Proofreading for Pronoun-Antecedent Errors

Proofread the following paragraph. When you find an error involving a pronoun and its agreement with its antecedent, cross the pronoun out. Then insert this proofreading symbol ∧ and write the correct pronoun or pronouns above it.

Jean Francois Gravelet, also known as Blondin, was a 19th-century daredevil. Many of his fellow tightrope walkers were content to ply his or her trade in traditional places such as a circus tent. Blondin, however, had other ideas. One of his stunts will always be remembered for their extreme recklessness. In 1859, Blondin had a cable strung across the Niagara River by the famous Falls. He was determined to walk on the cable from the American side to the Canadian side. No one else had ever risked their life in this way before.

When one takes their balancing pole and steps out over the roaring Falls, it makes news. All of the people in the crowd held their breath as Blondin began his stunt. For more than 17 minutes, Blondin carefully put each of his feet in front of their mate as he walked 190 feet above the river. None of the crowd could take its eyes off him. Finally, Blondin stepped onto solid ground. A new hero had been born.

B. Using Indefinite Pronouns in Writing

Write a story using at least four of these indefinite pronouns: *all, any, most, none, some.* Be sure that any personal pronouns agree with their indefinite pronoun antecedents in number.

_____

_____

_____

_____

_____

_____

_____

_____

For use with Pupil's Edition pp. 193–195

Lesson 7

Pronoun Reference Problems

Reteaching

The referent of a pronoun should always be clear.

Indefinite reference is a problem that occurs when the pronoun *it, you,* or *they* does not clearly refer to a specific antecedent. Fix this problem by rewording the sentence and eliminating the pronoun, or by replacing the pronoun with a noun.

Awkward	On the sign, it says that no hunting is allowed on the property.
Revised	The sign says that no hunting is allowed on the property.

A **general reference** problem occurs when the pronoun *it, this, that, which,* or *such* is used to refer to a general idea rather than to a specific antecedent. Fix the problem by rewriting the sentence.

Awkward	The dog will not obey its owners; this presents a big problem.
Revised	The dog's refusal to obey its owners presents a big problem.

An **ambiguous reference** problem occurs when a pronoun could refer to two or more antecedents. Eliminate the problem by rewriting the sentence to clarify what the pronoun refers to.

Awkward	Our cat and dog do not get along; she bothers him all the time.
Revised	Our cat and dog do not get along; the cat bothers the dog all the time.

Identifying Clear Pronoun References

In each pair of sentences below, one sentence has an indefinite, general, or ambiguous pronoun reference. The other is correct. Underline the sentence that is correct.

1. Clarise told her sister that the blouse was hers.
   Clarise told her sister that the blouse was her sister's.

2. Surgeons are using the latest medical equipment to do the operation.
   They are doing the operation using the latest medical equipment.

3. Because Ken visited China last year, he is familiar with the terra-cotta warriors.
   Ken visited China last year, which makes him familiar with the terra-cotta warriors.

4. On my ticket it says that my seats are in Row H.
   My ticket says my seats are in Row H.

5. Like most people, I hate spiders.
   I hate spiders. That is how most people feel.

6. The bus and the train both stop at this station. I just barely caught it today.
   The bus and the train both stop at this station. I just barely caught the bus today.

7. Steve tends to overplan his future, a habit that may cause him trouble one day.
   Steve tends to overplan his future, which may cause him trouble one day.

8. If they want to keep you dry, they should extend the porch over the front steps.
   If the homeowners want to keep their visitors dry, they should extend the porch over the front steps.

9. Manuel and Jason were playing baseball but Jason had to leave early.
   Manuel and Jason were playing baseball but he had to leave early.

Pronoun Reference Problems

More Practice

Avoiding Indefinite, General, and Ambiguous References

Rewrite the following sentences to correct indefinite, general, and ambiguous pronoun references. More than one interpretation may be possible. Add any words that are needed to make the meaning clear.

1. The wind is high today, which makes it a dangerous day for swimming.

_____

2. In the local newspapers it says snow is predicted.

_____

3. Before the concert, they set up their speakers.

_____

4. When the coach spoke to the referee, he was very calm.

_____

5. Our governor uses common sense to guide his decisions, which makes him an effective leader.

_____

6. At the back of the book, they list the writers and editors.

_____

7. Brian always protects his little brother John from bullies. That's why he stays close to him.

_____

8. As the story draws to an exciting conclusion, you find out the identity of the killer.

_____

9. I keep falling asleep while doing my homework. This has been a problem all year.

_____

10. The parents disagree with their children regarding the family vacation this year; they want to spend two weeks at the beach.

_____

11. According to this article, they are putting a school levy on the ballot in November.

_____

12. The aliens communicated directly into the brains of their human captives; they were connected with them at all times.

_____

For use with Pupil's Edition pp. 196–198

Pronoun Reference Problems   *Application*

A. Eliminating Pronoun Reference Problems

Revise the sentences below to correct all indefinite, general, or ambiguous pronoun reference problems. More than one interpretation may be possible.

1. On this Web site, they list the top ten jokes of the day.

_____

2. I took one orchid out of my corsage and then put it in the refrigerator.

_____

3. Jen always locks her bike with a strong lock, which is a good idea until you forget your key.

_____

4. I hate it when they show three long commercials in a row, which is why I hardly ever watch television.

_____

5. Sean moved his desk closer to the window and his bed across the room. He thinks it looks better that way.

_____

B. Using Clear Pronoun References

In the following paragraph, find the six sentences with indefinite, general, or ambiguous pronoun references. Revise the incorrect sentences on the lines below.

(1) Appearing in a movie is not always exciting. **(2)** They recently hired my cousin Theresa as an extra for the filming of *Nightmare in Flight*. **(3)** At first Theresa was speechless that she had been chosen, which is a rare occurrence in Theresa's life. **(4)** Theresa expected to meet glamorous stars, but it turned out to be a lot of dull waiting in an airport. **(5)** When Theresa did see the leading lady, she looked tired and cranky. **(6)** When they were finally ready, the director made the crew shoot the scene 12 times. **(7)** Maybe the lead actors were treated well, but the extras were ignored for hours. **(8)** Theresa said she was bored for much of the time. That's why she probably won't do it again.

_____

_____

_____

_____

_____

Lesson 8

Other Pronoun Problems

Reteaching

Pronouns can be used with an appositive, in an appositive, or in a comparison.

With an appositive An appositive is a noun or pronoun that follows another noun or pronoun for the purpose of identifying or explaining it. The pronouns *we* and *us* are often used with appositives. The nominative case, *we,* is used when the pronoun is a subject. The objective case, *us,* is used when the pronoun is an object.

> We fans waited outside the ballpark for the players.
> Pitcher Matt Gray gave us fans his autograph.

As an appositive A pronoun used as an appositive is in the case it would take if the noun were missing.

> The club officers, Bob and she, called the meeting to order.
> Members told the club officers, Bob and her, about committee news.

In a comparison A comparison can be made using *than* or *as* to begin a clause. When you omit some words from the final clause in a comparison, the clause is called **elliptical.** To determine the correct pronoun to use in an elliptical clause, mentally fill in the unstated words. Notice that the meaning you want to express can affect the choice of a pronoun.

> I like Bob better than she. (I like Bob more than she likes Bob.)
> I like Bob better than her. (I like Bob more than I like her.)

A. Choosing the Correct Pronoun

Underline the correct pronoun of the two given in parentheses.

1. (We, Us) students are electing student council officers.
2. Our teacher told (we, us) students to consider the qualifications of the candidates.
3. The top candidates, Ray and (him, he), are campaigning hard.
4. The principal chose two teachers, Mrs. Rosen and (he, him), as faculty advisors.
5. (We, Us) students are interested in the upcoming debate between the candidates, Neil and (he, him).
6. The candidates, Ray and (he, him), spoke briefly before the debate began.
7. Running the debate is the responsibility of the advisors, Mrs. Rosen and (he, him).
8. The poise of the speakers impressed all of (we, us) observers.
9. Both candidates, Neil and (he, him), answered the questions thoughtfully.
10. (We, Us) students now have a difficult decision to make.

B. Choosing the Correct Pronoun in Comparisons

Underline the correct pronoun of the two given in parentheses.

1. We are both interested in that report, but I am more interested than (she, her).
2. I hardly ever saw my cousin Tom growing up. In fact, I saw my uncle more than (he, him).
3. Mr. Boone was as brave as (she, her) during the long ordeal.
4. My sister is taller than (I, me), but people say I seem older.
5. They are as eager to go to the concert as (we, us).

For use with Pupil's Edition pp. 199–201

Lesson 8

Other Pronoun Problems

More Practice

A. Choosing the Correct Pronoun

Underline the correct pronoun of the two given in parentheses.

1. He is older than (I, me) by 12 years.

2. (We, Us) judges held up our scores after each dive.

3. Ms. Barton is similar to me in one way. She likes the novels of Charles Dickens as much as (I, me).

4. The contestants, Malcolm and (she, her), listened carefully to the first question.

5. The jury heard the closing statements of both attorneys, Ms. Franklin and (her, she).

6. My friend Kara is a better cook than (I, me).

7. The hostess showed (we, us) hungry people to our table.

8. The runners in the last race, Kelly and (I, me), waited for the starting gun.

9. If I could choose, I would rather meet George Washington than (him, he).

10. Your father is just as proud as (me, I) about your success.

11. (We, Us) campers prepared for the windstorm by securing our tent ropes.

12. Mrs. Richardson sometimes invites (we, us) neighborhood children into her house for cookies and milk.

B. Using Pronouns Correctly

Write an appropriate pronoun on the line in each sentence. Do not use the pronoun *you* or any possessive pronoun.

1. I am excited about my award, and my mother is as excited as _____ about it.

2. Donald can stay underwater longer than _____.

3. In all modesty, I must admit that no one sang better than _____.

4. _____ movie fans waited outside the box office for hours to buy tickets.

5. The main characters, Marsha and _____, were like me and my sister.

6. No one else on the stage was as funny as _____.

7. The lifeguard warned _____ swimmers that the water was rough today.

8. I like Richie Valens but not as much as _____; in other words, I like Buddy Holly better.

9. The two chefs, Mr. Lopez and _____, prepared a sumptuous feast.

10. You don't really need a stepladder, Mia; you are as tall as _____.

11. Your performance at the recital delighted _____ teachers.

CHAPTER 8

Lesson 8

Other Pronoun Problems

Application

A. Writing Elliptical Sentences Using Pronouns

Write an elliptical sentence with the same meaning as each of the following sentences. Replace the boldfaced noun with a pronoun. Use the correct pronoun to communicate your meaning.

> **EXAMPLE** Ray received more votes than **Neil** received.
> *Ray received more votes than he.*

1. The voters clearly liked Ray more than they liked **Neil.**

_____

2. Ray attended more class functions than **Neil** attended.

_____

3. Ray talked to more class members than **Neil** did.

_____

4. Would Neil have done a better job than **Ray** would have done?

_____

5. Some of the teachers believe that Neil is a harder worker than **Ray** is.

_____

6. The class officers worked harder for Ray than they did for **Neil.**

_____

B. Proofreading for Correct Pronoun Usage

Proofread the following paragraph. When you find a pronoun used incorrectly, cross it out. Then insert this proofreading symbol ∧ and write the correct pronoun above it.

     Us students just completed a comparison of local television news broadcasts. We have concluded that the news teams do a good job of communicating some news stories, but that they also underestimate and shortchange we viewers in one important way. The anchors on Channel A were likable and thorough. The anchors on Channel B were not as warm as them, but were better looking. On Channel C, the anchors are Tim and Ramona. Ramona gives the impression that on-site reporters have good rapport with the anchors, Tim and her. The problem is that none of the news teams report on issues of national or international interest, when such coverage is important for many viewers. We know that other viewers feel the same as us. Reporters in other cities, we suspect, are more comprehensive. Why can't our news teams be as thorough as them?

CHAPTER 8

Using Adjectives and Adverbs

Reteaching

Modifiers are words that give information about, or modify, the meanings of other words. Adjectives and adverbs are common modifiers. **Adjectives** modify nouns and pronouns. They answer the questions *which one?* (that, these) *what kind?* (small, funny) *how many?* (several, two) or *how much?* (enough, little).

Words classified as other parts of speech can be used as adjectives.

Nouns	<u>lead</u> pencil
Possessive Pronouns	<u>her</u> garden
Demonstrative Pronouns	<u>those</u> letters
Participles	<u>setting</u> sun, <u>wilted</u> flower

A **predicate adjective** follows a linking verb and modifies the subject of a clause.

> The peaches are <u>ripe</u>. (The adjective *ripe* modifies the noun *peaches*.)

Adverbs modify verbs, adjectives, and other adverbs. They answer the questions *where?* (away, west) *when?* (early, now) *how?* (carefully, slowly) and *to what degree?* (really, very).

Identifying Adjectives and Adverbs

Underline the adjectives once and the adverbs twice in these sentences. Do not underline articles or the names of the parks mentioned.

 1. Acadia National Park in Maine is a place of rugged beauty.
 2. I always enjoy the sight of the waves along the coast.
 3. A peaceful location like this often draws visitors back.
 4. Yosemite National Park has a different kind of beauty.
 5. Visitors to the western park see spectacular waterfalls and steep cliffs.
 6. The park has become very busy during the summer especially.
 7. Visitors can still get a peaceful experience by walking quietly and listening carefully to the sounds of nature.
 8. You find Isle Royale National Park in a remote area of Lake Superior.
 9. Most people reach the park on a ferry or a private boat.
10. In past years, miners discovered huge deposits of pure copper here, but now mining has ceased.
11. Wildlife, such as wolf and moose, roam freely about the park.
12. Usually the park attracts fit visitors who like to hike, since there are no roads on the island.
13. Visitors to Isle Royale should bring along powerful insect repellant.
14. The mosquitoes are extremely persistent.
15. Grand Canyon National Park has a truly international reputation.
16. Foreign tourists often make visiting the amazing park a high priority.
17. Once you have seen the Grand Canyon, you will never forget it.
18. A memory of quiet majesty will stay with you forever.
19. The government acted intelligently when it set the parks aside.
20. People will always appreciate natural splendor.

CHAPTER 9

Using Adjectives and Adverbs   *More Practice*

A. Identifying Adjectives and the Words They Modify

In each of the following sentences, underline the adjective once and the word it modifies twice. Do not underline articles or the name of the park.

1. The oldest park in the United States is Yellowstone National Park in Wyoming.
2. A geyser at the park erupts at regular intervals.
3. It makes a spectacular show when it erupts.
4. Visitors to Yellowstone always enjoy seeing the hot springs.
5. Water from the springs flows slowly through colorful terraces.
6. Because the park protects wildlife, animals are plentiful there.
7. Lofty mountains surround the park.
8. Visitors should definitely stop at the impressive waterfalls of the Yellowstone.
9. The water falls past the yellow walls of the canyon constantly and rapidly.
10. Yellowstone is a park of natural wonders.

B. Identifying Adverbs and the Words They Modify

Underline the word modified by each boldfaced adverb. Then in the blank after each sentence, tell the part of speech of the modified word. Write **V** for verb, **ADJ** for adjective, or **ADV** for adverb.

Last night the chorus sang **beautifully.** V

1. Denise spoke **confidently** about her project for psychology class. _____
2. This wing of the school is **completely** new and will open next month. _____
3. The savings account is **almost** depleted. _____
4. Martha behaved **somewhat** coldly toward her cousin. _____
5. He was **too** tired to watch the late-night comedy show. _____
6. She slammed the alarm clock **down** on the bureau and fell asleep. _____
7. Some writers and artists are **never** content with their own work. _____
8. The caterers **busily** set up the display table. _____
9. Julian touched the newborn kittens **so** gently that they purred. _____
10. Great athletes' performances often look **deceptively** simple. _____

Using Adjectives and Adverbs   *Application*

A. Writing Subjects and Predicates

Complete each of the following sentences by writing an adjective or an adverb in the blank within the sentence. Then write **ADJ** or **ADV** on the line at the right.

1. I have _____ traveled to Shenandoah National Park
   in Virginia.   _____

2. The park gives you _____ views of the
   Shenandoah Valley.   _____

3. Driving _____ along Skyline Drive, you encounter
   new beauty around every turn.   _____

4. The park has _____ hiking trails.   _____

5. Shenandoah is an easy day trip for visitors from _____
   cities, such as Baltimore, Maryland, and Washington, D.C.   _____

6. Look _____ in the spring, and you will see shy
   wildflowers blooming.   _____

B. Revising with Adjectives

Below is a description of a person. All the adjectives, except the articles, are in boldface. Create a new character. Rewrite the paragraph, and change the adjectives. Keep your adjectives consistent to describe the type of person you have in mind.

> The **tiny, slender** girl had **frizzy, red** hair and **hazel** eyes. "She must be about nine years old," I thought. She looked **sad** and **lonely.** She asked me the time. Was she **lost?** I couldn't tell.

_____

_____

_____

C. Revising with Adverbs

Below is a description of another person. All the adverbs are in boldface. Create a new character. Rewrite the paragraph, and change the adverbs. Keep your adverbs consistent to describe the type of person you have in mind.

> I **suddenly** spotted an unfamiliar man moving **slowly** and **gingerly** across the beach. He seemed to be looking **down** as he walked. He was repeating a few words **softly** as he approached. He spoke **seriously** and **intensely.**

_____

_____

_____

Problems with Modifiers

Reteaching

It's easy to confuse adjectives and adverbs. Many words have both adjective and adverb forms. In deciding whether to use an adverb or an adjective, follow these guidelines:

If you're not sure which form of a word to use, look at the word it modifies. If the modified word is a noun or pronoun, use the **adjective** form. If it's a verb, adjective, or adverb, use the **adverb** form.

Adjective	What is the <u>real</u> story? (*Real* modifies the noun *story*.)
Adverb	I need a <u>really</u> sharp pencil. (*Really* modifies the adjective *sharp*.)
Adjective	Adam feels <u>well</u>. (*Well* is a predicate adjective modifying the noun *Adam*.)
Adverb	Adam pitches <u>well</u>. (*Well* modifies the verb *pitches*.)
Adjective	Gina had a <u>bad</u> accident. (*Bad* modifies the noun *accident*.)
Adjective	Gina felt too <u>bad</u> to come to the dance. (*Bad* is a predicate adjective modifying the noun *Gina*.)
Adverb	Gina writes <u>badly</u> now that she is using her left hand. (*Badly* modifies the verb *writes*.)

Avoid using **double negatives**—two negative words in a single clause (nonstandard: I *don't* have *no* pencil).

Demonstrative adjectives—*this, that, these,* and *those* answer the question *which one?* Remember three rules when using these words as adjectives: (1) they must agree in number with the words they modify (*this* type, *these* kinds); (2) never use *here* or *there* with demonstrative adjectives (nonstandard: this *here* book); and (3) never use the pronoun *them* as an adjective in place of *these* or *those* (nonstandard: *them* students).

Using the Correct Modifier

Underline the correct word in parentheses in each sentence.

1. The blue jay clung (tightly, tight) to the branch throughout the storm.

2. The sun rose (real, really) early this morning.

3. Clara exercises (vigorous, vigorously) for 30 minutes every day.

4. Auto racing can be an (awful, awfully) dangerous sport.

5. Bill feels too (bad, badly) to go to school today.

6. The witness's story sounded (suspicious, suspiciously) to me.

7. Our puppy was sick yesterday, but he seems (well, good) today.

8. It seems (obvious, obviously) that Kim has been studying more.

9. Joellen looked (hilariously, hilarious) in her clown makeup.

10. Beth never wrote to (any, no) classmates this summer, despite her promise.

11. The rain poured down (steady, steadily) all day.

12. I would love a piece of (that, that there) peach pie.

13. Larry felt (bad, badly) about leaving his brother home alone.

14. Anita dances (good, well) enough to be a professional.

15. The toddler looked (wistful, wistfully) at the toys on the shelf.

For use with Pupil's Edition pp. 213–216

Problems with Modifiers

More Practice

A. Choosing the Correct Modifier

Underline the correct word in parentheses in each sentence.

   1. I felt (bad, badly) until the doctor put me on antibiotics.

   2. The geologist examined the rock (careful, carefully).

   3. (That, Those) kinds of jobs are always hard to land.

   4. Professional athletes must be (real, really) fit.

   5. Ed didn't (ever, never) consider farming as a career until now.

   6. After a good night's sleep, the mountain climber felt (good, well) enough
   to resume her attack on Mount Everest.

   7. The toddler cried (loud, loudly) until the babysitter picked her up.

   8. Her chicken salad tastes (delicious, deliciously) even on the second day.

   9. Students at that high school score (good, well) on standardized math tests.

 10. Lisa hasn't asked (no, any) teachers for references yet.

B. Choosing Between Adjectives and Adverbs

Underline once the correct word in parentheses in each sentence. Underline twice
the word it modifies.

   EXAMPLE The nurse <u>spoke</u> (pleasant, <u>pleasantly</u>) to the patient.

   1. Marian Anderson sang (beautiful, beautifully).

   2. Tanya is a (thoughtful, thoughtfully) person.

   3. Transmission fluid dripped (steady, steadily) from beneath the car.

   4. The elevator stopped (sudden, suddenly) between floors.

   5. This machine copies (quick, quickly).

   6. The vault opened (easy, easily), but there was nothing inside.

   7. Paul's description of the suspect was (accurate, accurately).

   8. Quinine water tastes (bitter, bitterly).

   9. Ice cream feels (soothing, soothingly) to a person with a sore throat.

 10. The defendant paced the floor (nervous, nervously).

 11. Marge reclined (lazy, lazily) on the beach towel.

 12. The laboratory technician checked the sample (careful, carefully).

 13. Dinner smells (wonderful, wonderfully) tonight.

 14. Nancy laughed (loud, loudly) throughout the movie.

 15. You seem (terrible, terribly) upset about the election.

Lesson 2

Problems with Modifiers

Application

A. Using Adjectives and Adverbs Correctly

Write sentences in which you correctly use the adjectives and adverbs given. Try to use verbs other than forms of be. Use action verbs or linking verbs such as *feel, seem, appear, become, taste, smell,* and *look.*

1. graceful _____

2. gracefully _____

3. bad _____

4. badly _____

5. natural _____

6. naturally _____

7. good _____

8. well _____

9. extreme _____

10. extremely _____

11. real _____

12. really _____

B. Writing with Adjectives and Adverbs

Proofread the following paragraph. When you find a modifier used incorrectly, cross it out. Then insert this proofreading symbol ∧ and write the correct modifier above it.

When you think about a future career, remember that everything worthwhile takes effort. Becoming a doctor isn't no exception. The path to the M.D. degree is long and difficult. There isn't no room for indecisive or unmotivated people in the field. After college, medical students study real intense for two full years. Then they work close with doctors in different fields for two more years. If they do good in all their classes and earn high grades, they can go on to the next step in the process—their residencies. For at least two more years, they can't hardly relax much because they are so busy. Residents are often real tired at the end of a long day or a long night on the job. These kinds of efforts finally pay off when doctors seek jobs. If they have done good in school and residencies, they have an excellent chance of landing good jobs.

For use with Pupil's Edition pp. 213–216

Using Comparisons

Reteaching

Adjectives and adverbs have two forms that can be used to make comparisons: the **comparative** form and the **superlative** form. The comparative form compares two persons, places, or things. The superlative form compares three or more persons, places, or things.

Adjectives
Comparative   The Sears Tower is <u>taller</u> than the Empire State Building.
Superlative   For years, the Sears Tower was the <u>tallest</u> building in the world.

Adverbs
Comparative   This printer responds <u>quicker</u> than the old one.
Superlative   This printer responds <u>quickest</u> of all the printers in the building.

Most modifiers are changed in regular ways to show comparisons. Add -*er* or -*est* to one syllable and many two-syllable words to form the comparative and superlative forms—add -*er* to form the comparative and -*est* to form the superlative (tough, tougher, toughest). Use *more* or *most* in these three instances: with some two-syllable words to avoid awkward sounds; with words of more than two syllables; and with adverbs ending in -*ly*.

Some modifiers have irregular comparative and superlative forms: *good, better, best; well, better, best; far, farther* or *further, farthest* or *furthest; bad, worse, worst; much, more, most; many, more, most; little, less* or *lesser, least*.

A. Identifying Comparative and Superlative Modifiers

Fill in the blank with **C** for comparative or **S** for superlative to identify the boldfaced modifier.

> **EXAMPLE**   Today, our city is **colder** than Anchorage, Alaska. *C*

1. The **most picturesque** town I have ever seen is in Vermont.   _____

2. The bus ride was the **longest** I've ever taken.   _____

3. Roberto thinks he can run **faster** than I can.   _____

4. Ethiopia has some of the **most magnificent** scenery in the world.   _____

5. Small, sporty cars sell **better** than large, luxury models.   _____

B. Using Modifiers in Comparisons

Study the boldfaced modifier in each of the following sentences. If the comparison is correct, write **Correct** on the line. If the comparison is incorrect, rewrite it correctly.

1. Who in our class is **more likely** to succeed?   _____

2. Charmaine dances **more gracefully** than I do.   _____

3. Who worked **hardest,** Roy or Jerome?   _____

4. Given her choice of the three techniques, Molly enjoys using watercolors **more.**   _____

5. The lake water is **muddier** than it was ten years ago.   _____

Lesson
3

Using Comparisons

More Practice

A. Using Modifiers in Comparisons

Study the boldfaced modifier in each of the following sentences. If the comparison is correct, write **Correct** on the line. If the comparison is incorrect, write the correct comparison on the line.

1. Of all the flutists, Suzanne was the **better.** _____

2. This painting is **more beautiful** than any of the others. _____

3. Bernie is the **funniest** person in our class. _____

4. You should take this situation **most seriously** than you have been. _____

5. I would like to sleep in the **sunnier** of these four bedrooms. _____

B. Using Comparisons

Underline the correct form of comparison for each sentence.

1. Which city is (more likely, most likely) to host the next Olympics?

2. Most reviewers rate our city's orchestra (higher, highest) than that of any other city in the country.

3. Which is the (busiest, busier) airport in the United States?

4. Which city's population is (greater, greatest), Chicago or Los Angeles?

5. Our city is (larger, largest) than it was ten years ago.

6. Of all the kindergarten children, who ran (faster, fastest) in the race?

7. Which mountain is (tallest, taller), Mount Everest, K-2, or Mount McKinley?

8. This freeway usually moves (more quickly, most quickly) than that one.

9. This waterfall falls (farther, farthest) than any other in the state.

10. Which Great Lake is the (most northerly, northerliest)?

11. Which of these two clocks tells time (more accurately, accurater)?

12. Which of these cities has the (fewest, most few) residents?

13. I have never swum in a (deepest, deeper) lake than this one.

14. Some people say that forests are at their (more beautiful, most beautiful) in the fall.

15. Blue Mountain is (more popular, most popular) than Green Mountain with hikers.

16. Which of these rivers runs (faster, most fast), the Mississippi or the Colorado?

17. (More, Most) travelers visit the seashore than any other vacation spot.

18. Ticket prices for the ballet are (more expensive, most expensive) than for the movies.

19. Today I feel (worse, worst) than I did yesterday.

20. The cheetah moves (fastest, faster) than any other animal alive.

21. Of all the items on the menu, the boiled fish appeals to me the (less, least).

22. Which is the (more populated, most populated) city on the face of the earth?

For use with Pupil's Edition pp. 217–219

CHAPTER 9

Lesson 3

Using Comparisons

Application

A. Using Comparisons in Sentences

Write sentences comparing the following items by using the comparative or the superlative form of the word in parentheses.

EXAMPLE one cup of cocoa compared with all other cups of cocoa (hot)
This is the hottest cup of cocoa I have ever tasted.

1. one comedian compared with two others (inventive)

_____

2. one book compared with another (riveting)

_____

3. one tree compared with all other trees in my yard (old)

_____

4. one golf course compared with another (difficult)

_____

5. one baseball pitcher compared with many others (fast)

_____

6. one board game compared with another (complex)

_____

B. Using Comparisons in Writing

Imagine that you have attended the Olympic Games as a spectator. You have seen several races and other competitions, and have even seen some world records broken. Write a letter about what you saw and heard. Include at least five comparative modifiers and five superlative modifiers.

_____
_____
_____
_____
_____
_____
_____
_____
_____

Lesson 4

Problems with Comparisons

Reteaching

When using modifiers to compare two or more things, writers may commit two errors: double comparisons and illogical comparisons.

Double Comparisons Do not use both *-er* and *more* to form a comparative. Do not use both *-est* and *most* to form a superlative.

Nonstandard	Mary Beth is the <u>most friendliest</u> girl in our class.
Standard	Mary Beth is the <u>friendliest</u> girl in our class.

Illogical Comparisons When you are comparing something that is part of a larger group to the group itself, use *other* or *else* to avoid an illogical comparison.

Nonstandard	To me, the telephone is more useful than <u>any invention</u>.
Standard	To me, the telephone is more useful than <u>any other invention</u>.

A. Using Comparisons Correctly

Underline the correct modifier in each sentence.

1. Alexander Graham Bell is (more famouser, more famous) than his assistant.

2. After Bell invented the telephone, people could communicate much (more easily, more easilier) than they could before.

3. Although he is (more better, better) known for the telephone, he also invented a method for teaching people with hearing problems.

4. Bell was (more curious, more curiouser) about sound than about any other subject.

5. He was (most excitedest, most excited) about using electricity to transmit speech.

6. Bell became a (greater, more greater) celebrity after he demonstrated his telephone at the 1876 Philadelphia Centennial.

7. Although his invention of the telephone is (better, more better) known, Bell also invented the audiometer, a machine that measures hearing ability.

8. Bell saved some of his (most inventivest, most inventive) ideas for the field of flight.

9. Bell invented the (most fastest, fastest) boat in the world, the hydrodrome.

10. People should be (most gratefulest, most grateful) to Bell for his intense curiosity.

B. Using Comparisons Correctly

In each pair of sentences, underline the sentence that uses modifiers correctly.

> **EXAMPLE** a. The automobile is more useful than any invention.
> b. <u>The automobile is more useful than any other invention.</u>

1. a. Most inventors are more stubborn than anyone.

   b. Most inventors are more stubborn than anyone else.

2. a. Where any other human being would see an impossible situation, they see a challenge.

   b. Where any human being would see an impossible situation, they see a challenge.

3. a. More than anyone, inventors think "outside the box."

   b. More than anyone else, inventors think "outside the box."

For use with Pupil's Edition pp. 220–221

Problems with Comparisons

More Practice

A. Using Comparisons Correctly

Underline the correct modifier in each sentence.

1. My computer is (more easier, easier) to use than this one.
2. Which computer chip is the (most fastest, fastest)?
3. I prefer a (sharper, more sharper) screen than this one.
4. The newest modems work (quicker, more quicker) than ones from a year ago.
5. Laptop computers are being made even (more lighter, lighter) than before.

B. Correcting Double Comparisons and Illogical Comparisons

Rewrite any sentence that contains comparison errors. If you find a comparison error, write the sentence correctly on the line below it. If a sentence contains no error, write **Correct.**

1. In this day and age, we have many more labor-saving devices than any generation ever had.

   _____

2. Today, people can sew more faster with a sewing machine than they can by hand.

   _____

3. Perhaps we should be more grateful to Thomas Edison than to anyone else.

   _____

4. Who hasn't found Edison's electric light bulb more usefuler than any invention?

   _____

5. His motion picture projector did more to change entertainment than any single invention.

   _____

6. Some people think that, more than anyone, he ushered in the modern era.

   _____

7. He is considered to have had one of the most creativest minds of his time.

   _____

8. His automatic telegraph system made the telegraph work with even greater speed than before.

   _____

9. No one else thought of his invention that improved the telephone—the carbon transmitter.

   _____

10. I wonder what he would choose as his most importantest invention.

    _____

Problems with Comparisons

Application

A. Proofreading for Comparison Errors

The following paragraph contains several errors involving comparisons. When you find a modifier used incorrectly, cross it out. Then insert this proofreading symbol ∧ and write the correct modifier above it.

Charles Goodyear may have been the most unluckiest of all inventors. His first stroke of bad luck occurred when he entered into a partnership with his father in a hardware business. The venture was least successful than they hoped it would be. The business eventually failed, and Goodyear was forced to find a new way to make a living. A naturally curious man, he became fascinated with the possibility of finding a way to make rubber less brittle. Perhaps Goodyear took the challenge of discovery more seriously than anyone, experimenting for years while his family lived in poverty. He had heard that adding sulfur might help make rubber more flexibler, and he pursued that possibility for quite a while. Unfortunately, his experiments were unsuccessful for years. Then one day he accidentally dropped both rubber and sulfur on a hot stove. The heat gave the rubber-sulfur mixture qualities more closer to those Goodyear was looking for. He was overjoyed with his good fortune, no matter how overdue it was. However, after his great discovery, Goodyear had even more worser luck than before. More cleverer competitors stole his ideas, and he died poor.

B. Using Comparisons in Writing

Imagine you are a television critic who is reviewing all the new shows that are beginning this year. You see similarities and differences among programs. You compare the characters, settings, and plots of many different shows. Write the review article below. Use at least six comparative and superlative modifiers to compare the fictional fall lineup of shows with programs that really are on the air today. Use a separate piece of paper if needed.

_____

_____

_____

_____

_____

_____

For use with Pupil's Edition pp. 220–221

People and Nationalities

Reteaching

People's names and titles, the names of the languages they speak, and the religions they practice are all proper nouns and should be capitalized. Capitalize these words and the following:

- people's names and initials that stand for names *Example:* John F. Kennedy
- people's titles and abbreviations for titles *Example:* General Patton, Gen. Patton
- abbreviations of some titles when they follow names *Example:* Inez Garcia, Ph.D.
- title of royalty or nobility only when it precedes a person's name
  Example: Queen Anne
- words indicating family relationships only when they are used as parts of names or in direct address *Example:* Uncle Ed
- the pronoun "I"
- names of ethnic groups, races, languages, and nationalities, along with adjectives formed from those names *Example:* American
- names of religions, religious denominations, sacred days, sacred writings, and deities *Examples:* Christianity, Rosh Hashanah, Allah

Capitalizing Names of People and Nationalities

Underline the letters that should be capitalized in each of the following sentences. If the sentence is already correct, write **Correct.**

1. Prime Minister Winston Churchill was both a statesman and a writer. _____

2. Did general dwight d. eisenhower lead the United States forces in Korea? _____

3. My grandfather knew Dr. Martin Luther King, Jr., the famous civil rights leader. _____

4. Clara Barton served as a volunteer nurse during the Civil War. _____

5. Alexander graham bell was born to a scottish family. _____

6. My mother thinks bell was the greatest american inventor. _____

7. The traveling circus was pioneered by p. t. barnum. _____

8. His circus provided a stage for the great singer, jenny lind. _____

9. The holy day of yom kippur falls in the seventh month of the jewish year. _____

10. Margaret thatcher was a very popular leader. _____

11. Hoping to have a male heir, king henry VIII married anne boleyn. _____

12. The vast roman Empire was ruled by julius caesar. _____

13. The egyptian queen, cleopatra, was his ally. _____

14. Joseph Smith was the founder of Mormonism. _____

15. The mayor of our town is interested in the work of dr. jonas b. salk. _____

16. Did grandma johnson visit the summer home of inventor thomas edison in Florida? _____

CHAPTER 10

Lesson 1

People and Nationalities

More Practice

A. Capitalizing Names of People and Nationalities

Underline the letters that should be capitalized in each of the following sentences. If the sentence is already correct, write **Correct.**

1. The french military leader napoleon bonaparte was a military genius. _____

2. Didn't aunt clarice collect souvenirs of european history? _____

3. She is especially interested in swiss cuckoo clocks because her ancestors come from switzerland. _____

4. Social activist Jane Addams helped Chicago immigrants learn the English language. _____

5. The explorer meriwether lewis opened the way for growth in America. _____

6. He and his partner, william clark, led an expedition across the country. _____

7. The presbyterian church was established by john knox. _____

8. The legend of pocahontas and captain john smith is part of american folklore. _____

9. The Congo in Africa became the home of scottish adventurer dr. david livingston. _____

10. Sir Edmund P. Hillary was the first to reach the top of Mt. Everest in 1953. _____

11. Followers of christianity observe a season of repentance called lent in preparation for their easter celebration. _____

12. Sitting bull and his sioux warriors defeated general george a. custer. _____

13. In 1945, President Harry Truman made the decision to drop the atom bomb. _____

14. Tending to the sick and dying, mother theresa was a missionary to the poor in india. _____

15. One of the most dangerous men in history was adolf hitler, the german dictator. _____

B. Capitalizing Correctly

Underline each letter that should be capitalized in the following paragraph.

　　　Some of the most influential people in modern history have been presidents of the United States. The first leader of our country was president george washington, who led the colonists in their war against king george. He and the other early presidents, such as john adams, thomas jefferson, and james madison, helped to establish our government. Later leaders, most notably abraham lincoln, worked to preserve our nation. President woodrow wilson and president franklin d. roosevelt presided over our country during wartime. Today, american presidents continue to wield great power around the world.

For use with Pupil's Edition pp. 230–232

CHAPTER 10

People and Nationalities
Application

A. Proofreading

Proofread the following first draft of a report. Look especially for errors in capitalization. Draw three lines under each letter that should be capitalized. Draw a slash across any letter that is capitalized when it should be lowercased.

EXAMPLE My *f*ather is an expert in european history.

Born in France in the early 1400s, joan of arc was a remarkable young woman. Her Country was fighting a terrible war against England when joan heard a divine Call to help. She led the armies of king charles VII into battle against the english troops. Her grateful king Honored her highly. This respect was not long-lasting, however, because the very next year Joan disobeyed King Charles and followed god instead of the king. Captured by the english, she was tried as a heretic for defying the roman catholic church. Charles made no attempt to save her. Joan of arc was burned at the stake as a heretic. Twenty-five years later, joan's Conviction was overturned. Much later, the church pronounced her saint joan. People to this day are inspired by the courage of this young french girl.

B. Writing with Capital Letters

Suppose that you are asked to lead a group around a wax museum that features wax statues of famous people from history. Write a short speech that you might give on your tour. Include at least ten words that need capitalization, such as names of people, personal titles, family relationships, the pronoun *I*, and the names of ethnic groups or nationalities.

_____
_____
_____
_____
_____
_____
_____
_____

Lesson 2

First Words and Titles   *Reteaching*

Use capital letters to begin the following words:

- the first word of every sentence and of every line of traditional poetry
- the first word of a direct quotation if it is a complete sentence (Do not capitalize a direct quotation if it is a fragment of a sentence. In a divided quotation, do not capitalize the first word of the second part of the quotation unless it starts a new sentence.)
- the first word of the greeting and of the closing of a letter
- the first word of each entry in an outline as well as the letters that introduce major subsections
- the first, last, and all other important words in titles; but not conjunctions, articles, or prepositions of fewer than five letters

Capitalizing First Words and Titles

Underline the words that should be capitalized in each of the following items. If the item is capitalized correctly, write **Correct** on the line.

1. dear Ms. Taylor:

   please send me two tickets for your lecture on May 12.

   sincerely yours,   _____

2. One of shakespeare's characters says, "all the world's a stage."   _____

3. loveliest of trees, the cherry now

   is hung with bloom along the bough,

   and stands about the woodland ride

   wearing white for Eastertide.

   —A. E. Housman, from *A Shropshire Lad*   _____

4. have you read the article "biking, past and present" in *cycle?*

5. two of my favorite short stories are "sixteen" and "strawberry ice cream soda."   _____

6. ms. Cass exclaimed, "you should have seen the Viking exhibit at the museum!"   _____

7. *The Outsiders* and other books by S. E. Hinton are popular with students. _____

8. *"The King and I,"* I told Julie, "is my favorite film."   _____

9. anne Frank wrote, "i still believe that people are really good at heart."   _____

10. "that was a great movie," said Tom. "now let's have something to eat."   _____

11. Jonathan subscribes to the magazine *Your Car.*   _____

12. The English class will go to see *fiddler on the roof* at the community theater. _____

13. "come on over when you get through with your work, Trish," shouted Mandy.   _____

14. "I can't believe it!" muttered Jeff. "The car is out of gas."   _____

  For use with Pupil's Edition pp. 233–235

First Words and Titles

More Practice

A. Capitalizing First Words and Titles

Underline the words that contain capitalization errors in the following items.

1. "baa, baa, black sheep, have you any wool?" begins a well-known nursery rhyme.

2. we are to read *wuthering heights* for our next assignment.

3. the audience clapped along to the rousing march "stars and stripes forever."

4. my class schedule
   I. morning classes
      a. world history
      b. algebra
   II. afternoon classes
      a. english
      b. art

5. "I can't come this afternoon," said Jackson, "Because I have to work at the store."

6. "my mom would be glad to bring cookies to the youth meeting," offered Sheila.

7. mrs. Murphy asked, "can you deliver the flowers to the hospital?"

8. dear Karen,

   thank you so much for the beautiful bracelet. it will be just right to wear for the prom. you were so thoughtful to lend it to me.

   your Friend,

9. Larisa enjoyed the movie playing at local theaters, *prom night.*

10. "give me your best guess," prompted Mr. Dade. "think about what you just read."

B. Capitalizing First Words in Letters

Underline each letter that should be capitalized in the following letter. Rewrite the letter on the lines below.

dear Carla,
we are anxious to see you next week. maybe we can go to see the new movie *you said what?* have you heard anything about it? it is supposed to be pretty funny. since it is based on the book *whatever made you say that?,* it should be! when my sister was reading it, I heard her laughing all the time. no matter what we do, we'll have a great time, I'm sure.

love,

_____

_____

_____

_____

First Words and Titles

Application

A. Writing a Letter

Write a letter to a friend in which you describe any books, plays, short stories, or poems you are reading in English class. Include at least one imaginary quotation from a teacher or another student. Use traditional letter format. Be sure to capitalize correctly.

_____

_____

_____

_____

_____

_____

_____

_____

B. Writing an Outline Using Capital Letters Correctly

Read the following brief report. Then write a short outline of it on the lines below. Be sure to capitalize correctly.

The Stone Age can be divided into two different periods: the Paleolithic Age, or Old Stone Age, and the Neolithic Age, or New Stone Age.

During these ages, humans invented tools, mastered fire, began to communicate, and began to control the environment.

_____

_____

_____

_____

_____

_____

_____

For use with Pupil's Edition pp. 233–235

Lesson
3

Places and Transportation

Reteaching

CHAPTER 10

The names of specific places, celestial bodies, landmarks, and vehicles are capitalized. Capitalize:

- each word in a geographical name except articles and prepositions *Example:* Isle of Wight
- the words *north, south, east,* and *west* when they name particular regions of the country or world, or are parts of proper names *Example:* West Coast
- names of planets and other specific objects in the universe (Only capitalize *earth* when it is used with other astronomical terms. Do not capitalize *earth* when it is preceded by the article the or when it refers to land or soil. Do not capitalize *sun* or *moon.*)
- names of specific buildings, bridges, monuments, and other landmarks *Example:* Statue of Liberty
- names of specific airplanes, trains, ships, cars, and spacecraft *Example:* the *Orient Express*

Capitalizing Names of Places and Transportation Modes

Underline the words that should be capitalized in each of the following sentences. If the item is capitalized correctly, write **Correct** on the line.

1. Red beans and rice is a traditional louisiana dish. _____

2. The wind is traveling northwest at 60 miles per hour. _____

3. Two of hawaii's beautiful islands are maui and kauai. _____

4. As you might guess, the finger lakes in new york are long and narrow. _____

5. Parts of the ohio river sometimes freeze over. _____

6. Did you know that chicago is the largest city in the midwest? _____

7. Many fault lines run through areas of the West Coast. _____

8. Potomac park in washington, d.c., is the site of the lincoln memorial. _____

9. If you are standing at the north pole, the only direction to go is south. _____

10. The strait of gibraltar links the atlantic ocean with the mediterranean sea. _____

11. Composed of volcanic rock, the Klamath Mountains are located in Oregon. _____

12. Native Americans built the adena burial mounds in west virginia. _____

13. The assassination of Martin Luther King, Jr., is commemorated by the national civil rights museum in memphis, tennessee. _____

14. U.S. spacecraft *voyager I* photographed the rings of jupiter. _____

15. The sea of galilee receives water from the jordan river. _____

16. Hilton Head Island lies off the coast of South Carolina. _____

Places and Transportation

More Practice

CHAPTER 10

A. Capitalizing Names of Places and Transportation Modes in Sentences

Underline the words that should be capitalized in each of the following sentences. If the item is capitalized correctly, write **Correct** on the line.

1. On a vacation in the American west you can see spectacular desert sunsets. _____

2. Carlsbad caverns in new mexico is an impressive natural wonder of the southwest. _____

3. Reservations are required for camping at yellowstone national park. _____

4. The black hills of south dakota contain countless fossils. _____

5. The Gulf of Mexico is the largest gulf in the world. _____

6. Lake michigan is the only one of the great lakes entirely within the united states. _____

7. The upper peninsula of michigan is home to several quaint towns. _____

8. Since no cars are allowed on Mackinac Island, buggies and bicycles are the favored mode of transportation. _____

9. Vacationers ride burros to the bottom of the grand canyon. _____

10. The swallows return to the mission at san juan capistrano every year on March 15. _____

11. The small town of avalon welcomes visitors to catalina island. _____

12. Paleontologists gain insights into Ice Age animals at the la brea tar pits. _____

13. Athletes do incredible dives off the cliffs of la quebrada in acapulco, mexico. _____

14. The building of hoover dam created man-made lake mead. _____

15. Most of Nevada is included in an area called the Great Basin. _____

B. Capitalizing Names of Places in a Paragraph

Underline each letter that should be capitalized in the following paragraph.

The capital of the united states is washington, d.c. It is also known as "The district" or "d.c." The potomac river separates the district of columbia from its neighbors, virginia and maryland. Historic georgetown lies on the banks of the potomac. Since d.c. has a height limit for buildings, crystal city was built in arlington, virginia. From this high-rise complex there is a view of landmarks such as the capitol, the jefferson memorial, and the towering washington monument. The washington monument is an obelisk set in the national mall, a parklike area that stretches from capitol hill west to the lincoln memorial. Tourists know this area well, and many visit the smithsonian institution buildings there.

For use with Pupil's Edition pp. 236–238

Places and Transportation

Application

A. Proofreading for Capital Letters

Read the following friendly letter about a vacation. Draw three lines under any letters that should be capitalized but are not. Draw a slash across any letter that is capitalized incorrectly.

EXAMPLE My aunt and I took the best trip to the B̸eaches of e̲u̲r̲o̲p̲e̲.

(1) To my World-traveling Aunt Marilyn,

(2) I want to thank you again for taking me with you on your Trip to Europe. **(3)** Imagine me, traveling on the concorde to london's heathrow airport! **(4)** And I never expected to sail on the *majesty III* to the Ports of provence! **(5)** It was truly a dream come true to find myself on the beautiful riviera. **(6)** Our day in marseilles was so much fun. **(7)** I'm not sure whether I enjoyed that day or our visit to genoa, italy, more. **(8)** Since I've flown home across the atlantic ocean, I've been remembering the clear blue waters of the gulf of genoa and its bright Beaches. **(9)** Here in iowa, the gold of the cornfields takes my imagination quickly back to that warm sand. **(10)** Everything around me is a reminder of our great trip to the mediterranean sea.

B. Using Capital Letters in Writing

Imagine that you are keeping a journal about a trip from Cape Canaveral, Florida, to the planet Pluto. Write a journal entry below. Mention at least two names from each of these categories: geographical names (could be imaginary); names of planets or other objects in the universe; specific monuments or landmarks; and names of airplanes, trains, ships, or aircraft.

_____

_____

_____

_____

_____

_____

_____

_____

_____

Lesson 4

Organizations and Other Subjects

Reteaching

Use capital letters for the following:

- all important words in names of organizations, institutions, stores, and companies *Example:* University of Virginia
- abbreviations of the names of organizations and institutions *Example:* AMA (American Medical Association)
- names of historical events, periods, and documents *Example:* the Mayflower Compact
- the abbreviations B.C., A.D., A.M., and P.M.
- names of months, days, and holidays, but not the seasons *Example:* Fourth of July
- names of special events and awards *Example:* World Series
- brand names of products but not common nouns that follow brand names *Example:* Supercrunch cereal
- names of school subjects only when they refer to specific courses, plus any proper nouns and adjectives that are part of the name *Example:* Physics II
- the word *freshman, sophomore, junior, or senior* when it is used as a proper noun or in a direct address

Identifying Correct Capitalization

Underline the letters that should be capitalized in each of the following sentences. If the sentence is correct, write **Correct.**

1. A member of the international red cross spoke at mayfield high school. _____

2. The first olympic games were held in 776 B.C. _____

3. The American society for the prevention of cruelty to animals (aspca) was formed in 1866. _____

4. The future teachers of america will have a conference at the university of oklahoma. _____

5. Parkwood high school's football team will host a speaker from the nfl. _____

6. The french club field trip is scheduled to leave at 8:00 A.M. _____

7. Do you have money to buy cookies from the girl scouts? _____

8. The house of representatives will vote today on the medicare act. _____

9. The uso provided comfort and relief to the soldiers of world war II. _____

10. The junior class serves turkey dinners on Thanksgiving Day. _____

11. Our summer vacation ends just before labor day. _____

12. The girl's volleyball team will play at 5:00 P.M. at mount washington high school. _____

13. The economics I class is charting the daily closings on the nasdaq. _____

Lesson 4 Organizations and Other Subjects

More Practice

A. Capitalizing Names of Organizations and Other Subjects

Underline each letter that should be capitalized in the following sentences.

1. The boy scouts of america was founded as a service organization for young men.
2. The choir of the manhattan school of music performed works by George Gershwin.
3. *The Story of Mankind,* written in 1922, was the first book to win the newbery medal.
4. Are you taking biology 2, advanced placement world history, and german?
5. The cleveland clinic is known worldwide for its medical expertise.
6. Serfs served their lords during the middle ages.
7. The industrial revolution is still continuing in some parts of the world.
8. Each year pulitzer prizes are awarded for achievement in journalism, literature, and music.
9. Belle is particularly interested in woven art from the renaissance.
10. Courageous world war II aviator James Doolittle was awarded the medal of honor.
11. My mother always buys squeeky kleen detergent when it's on sale.
12. Recruiters from the university of arizona phoned our star player yesterday.

B. Capitalizing Correctly

Read this paragraph. Then underline the words in each sentence that should be capitalized.

(1) Franklin D. Roosevelt high school provides plenty of activities for its students. (2) You can try out for sports teams such as our football team, the fighting tigers. (3) Our golf team caddies at the marshalltown invitational tournament every year, meeting many well-known professional golfers. (4) Academic clubs, such as the future scientists of america, offer opportunities for both fun and learning. (5) For example, the fsa is planning a spring trip to the nasa space center in Cape Canaveral, Florida. (6) Or perhaps the choir's trip to the renaissance music festival sounds inviting to you. (7) Many students choose to participate in the service projects of the key club. (8) Its members have joined with the members of the aarp in service to housebound elderly. (9) So get involved, freshmen! (10) Roosevelt high school has a place for you.

Organizations and Other Subjects

Application

A. Proofreading for Capitalization Errors

Read the following minutes from a meeting of a school extracurricular activities club. Draw three lines under any letters that should be capitalized but are not. Draw a slash across any letter that is capitalized incorrectly.

EXAMPLE Palomino <u>h</u>igh <u>s</u>chool holds all C̸lub meetings on Thursday afternoon.

The junior classical league of palomino high school met thursday afternoon, April 6. The president called the Meeting to order at 3:45 P.M. and requested that the Secretary read the minutes. The minutes included a report on some old Business, the Carnival fundraising Project. The palomino police department sent a note of thanks for our club's help in organizing this event. New business discussed was the upcoming Trip to the Latin festival to be held at the University Of Pittsburgh in June. Three more chaperones from the parent advisory board must be found. The jcl meeting was adjourned at 4:30 P.M.

B. Using Capitalization in Writing

Imagine that you are the publicity chairperson for a school club whose acronym is SWAMP. Write a newspaper notice about your club's next meeting, inviting others to attend. Include at least one of each of the following:

the full name of an organization
a time abbreviation
a product's name
a date or holiday

the name of a building
an award or special event
a course name

_____

_____

_____

_____

_____

_____

_____

_____

_____

_____

For use with Pupil's Edition pp. 239–241

Lesson 1

Periods and Other End Marks

Reteaching

End marks are used to indicate the end of sentences. Use a period at the end of all declarative sentences, most imperative sentences, and most indirect questions.

Declarative sentence	Japan is a country of islands.
Imperative sentence	Tell me about the history of Japan.
Indirect question	Jon asked how the rate of currency exchange is set.

Use a **period** after an abbreviation or an initial. *Example:* Mrs. Helen T. West

Use a **period** after each number and letter in an outline or list.

Use a **question mark** at the end of an interrogative sentence.

Interrogative sentence Where is Japan located?

Use an **exclamation point** to end an exclamatory sentence or after a strong interjection.

Exclamatory sentence What a beautiful mountain!

Using Periods and Other End Marks

Add punctuation as necessary in the following items.

1. Have you ever visited Japan
2. Japan has more people per square mile than most countries in the world
3. Imagine 126 million people in an area roughly the size of the state of Montana
4. By comparison, Montana has fewer than one million residents
5. How crowded Japan must be
6. Japan had been influenced by Chinese culture from about A D 400
7. American Commodore Matthew C Perry sailed into Tokyo Bay in 1853
8. Nancy asked how Perry was welcomed in this land that desired isolation
9. How do you think they would have reacted if Perry hadn't come on a warship
10. Japan enthusiastically modernized its industries during the 1870s
11. What an outpouring of energy there must have been
12. I wonder how they accomplished that feat so quickly
13. Japan grew as an economic power through the early 1900s
14. How did Japan overcome the effects of World War II
15. How devastating the atom bomb was
16. I   The 1500s
    A Arrival of the Europeans
    B Beginning of trade with Europe
    C Arrival of Christian missionaries in Japan
    II The period between 1850 and 1900
    A Arrival of Commodore Perry from U S A
    B Drive to modernize Japanese industries

CHAPTER 11

Periods and Other End Marks

More Practice

A. Using End Marks

Add punctuation marks where necessary in the following sentences.

1. The defense attorney asked the witness for the prosecution if he had ever seen the defendant before
2. Hooray The Blue Sox won the championship
3. Can you name some individuals who fought in the Spanish-American War
4. Dr Roger Harmon's specialty is sports medicine
5. In Great Britain tea is served at around 5:00 P M
6. Can't you read the sign posted over there
7. Did you know that Jerome has been named to the city all-star team
8. Truman defeated John E Dewey in the 1948 presidential election
9. Tell me where I should plant the geraniums and azaleas
10. Have you heard the weather forecast for this weekend
11. I   British political parties
    A Conservative Party
    B Labour Party
    C Liberal Party
    D Social Democratic Party
12. Look There's a landslide on that mountain
13. Oh Is today their anniversary
14. Jennifer asked for the number of the J D Cohen Furniture Company
15. Ask Jamal whether the bus leaves at 1:00 or at 2:00 P M

B. Using End Marks in Writing

Add periods, question marks, and exclamation points where necessary in the following paragraph.

(1) Which religions play a role in Japanese life (2) Shinto, an ancient religion, has had an influence on Japanese culture since prehistoric times (3) What does Shinto teach (4) Shintoists believe in gods that reside in all aspects of nature (5) Buddhism is a religion that encourages its followers to live a life of virtue and wisdom (6) How happy the smiling Buddha looks (7) What other religions do the Japanese people follow (8) Some Japanese are Christians, while others follow the moral teachings of Confucianism

For use with Pupil's Edition pp. 250–251

Periods and Other End Marks

Application

A. Using End Marks in Writing

Add periods, question marks, and exclamation points where necessary in the following paragraph. To add a period, insert this symbol ⊙. To add a question mark or an exclamation point, use a caret ∧ and write the correct punctuation mark above it.

Traditional theater in Japan is very different from that of contemporary United States For example, in the *No* play developed around A D 1300, actors all wear masks What is the function of the chorus in the *No* play It emphasizes and repeats important lines from the play If you were to see a *No* play, you would say, "How strange and stylized the movements of the actors are" Another traditional type of play in Japan is the *Kabuki* play, which evolved from the *No* theater In *Kabuki,* actors wear lots of makeup and move about the stage in a grand, exaggerated way How different from modern plays these ancient forms are Aren't you glad that they have survived for centuries

B. Using End Marks in an Outline

Think about your life so far. Divide it into three main periods. Then write a short outline about it. Give the outline a title, and write the three main ideas and two details for each main idea on the outline form below. Be sure to punctuate correctly.

Title: _____

I   _____

   A _____

   B _____

II   _____

   A _____

   B _____

III _____

   A _____

   B _____

Commas in Sentence Parts

Reteaching

In a series of three or more, use a comma after every item in the series except the last one.

> They grow beans, peas, and squash in their garden.

Use a comma after *first, second,* and so on when they introduce a series.

> Follow these steps when preparing your garden: first, turn the soil over; second, break it up; and third, plant the seeds.

Use a comma between two or more adjectives of equal rank that modify the same noun.

> I hope to make healthful, nutritious meals from my garden produce.

Use a comma after introductory words or mild interjections such as *oh, yes, no,* and *well.*

Use a comma after an introductory prepositional phrase that contains additional prepositional phrases.

> At the break of day, I water my flowers.

Use a comma after verbal phrases and adverb clauses that are used as introductory elements.

> After the storm ended, I examined the damage to my crops.

Use commas to set off one or more words that interrupt the flow of thought in a sentence.

> Tending a garden, I believe, improves my mental health.

Use commas to set off nouns of direct address.

> Doug, go pick some tomatoes for a salad.

Use commas to set off nonessential appositives.

> My youngest sister, Amy, helps me weed my garden.

Using Commas Correctly

Insert commas where necessary in the following sentences.

1. Dickens's character Ebenezer Scrooge was a mean stingy old man.
2. Your paper must include the following: first an outline; second three to five pages of text; third endnotes; and fourth a bibliography.
3. Emily's favorite poets are Alice Walker Gwendolyn Brooks and Anne Sexton.
4. Yes I would be delighted to come to your party.
5. Picnickers brought sandwiches potato salad lemonade and fruit.
6. After the concert ended the audience asked for three encores.
7. In our tent beside the river we enjoyed a peaceful night's sleep.
8. Pay close attention Carolyn while I show you how to crochet.
9. Sulfur has a strong unpleasant smell.
10. My favorite rock group the Creed is appearing tonight at the Odeon.
11. Examining the ground for shells we slowly made our way down the beach.

For use with Pupil's Edition pp. 252–254

Lesson 2

Commas in Sentence Parts

More Practice

A. Using Commas

Underline the words in each sentence that should be followed by a comma.

1. I am planting radishes cucumbers and beans this year.

2. My next-door neighbor Ed is loaning me a tiller for turning over the soil.

3. Kathy when is the best time to plant peas?

4. Well I never plant them until after the last frost.

5. You must remember of course that I am no expert at gardening.

6. When my garden is finally in I will just sit back and relax.

7. I will wait for the fresh delicious vegetables to make their appearance.

8. First the peas will bloom; second the tomatoes will appear; and third the eggplant will be ready.

9. In the fall I will turn over the soil again.

10. My friend Grace will help me can tomato sauce.

B. Using Commas in Writing

Rewrite the following paragraph, using commas where they are needed.

Microorganisms include bacteria yeasts and molds. They are tiny invisible creatures. Whether you can see them or not they are on your hands inside your body and in the air. Many microorganisms are harmful, but some can be useful. First molds are used to make antibiotics other medicines and cheeses. Second yeasts are used for making breads synthetic vitamins and some beverages. Third bacteria are sometimes used in food products. To make yogurt for example you need two types of bacteria. Actually whether you like it or not microorganisms are part of your world.

_____

_____

_____

_____

_____

_____

_____

_____

CHAPTER 11

Commas in Sentence Parts   *Application*

A. Writing with Complete Subjects and Complete Predicates

Add commas where they are needed in the following paragraph. Use the proofreading symbol ⌄.

      Yes it's true. I have decided to become a vegetarian. Why have I made this decision? First I think that eating meat is not healthy for me. Second I object to the amount of the earth's resources that are required to produce meats as opposed to vegetables. Third I object to eating meat on moral grounds. I don't eat beef pork poultry or seafood. For example I won't even eat crab salad. When I am at a party I always check to see what the ingredients in the food are. I follow a clear easy-to-understand rule: if it can look back at me I don't eat it. When I sit down at my favorite restaurant the Square Meal I can be sure that the food that comes my way is nonmeat healthful and delicious.

B. Using Commas in Writing

Rewrite the sentences by following the directions in parentheses.

1. They packed for the journey. (Include a series of items.)

_____

_____

2. This was to be an adventure. (Include two adjectives of equal rank that modify the same noun.)

_____

_____

3. They wanted to experience the thrill; they wanted to test themselves. (Include first and second to introduce a series.)

_____

_____

4. The adventure was a memorable experience for many reasons. (Include a series of reasons.)

_____

_____

5. They met their major goal. (Include a nonessential appositive.)

_____

_____

    For use with Pupil's Edition pp. 252–254

Name _____ Date _____

Lesson 3

More Commas

Reteaching

Use a comma whenever the reader might otherwise be confused.

> After the war, veterans paraded down Main Street.

Use commas to set off a direct quotation from explanatory words such as *she said* or *Pat suggested*.

> "I'd like to help," she said, "by decorating the float."

Use a comma before the conjunction that joins the two independent clauses in a compound sentence.

> The parade begins at the town square, and it ends at the War Memorial.

Use commas to set off nonessential clauses.

> The high school band, which performed at the state fair, will march.

Use a comma after the salutation and the closing of a friendly letter.

Use a comma between the day of the month and the year (and after the year in a sentence), between the name of a city and state or country and after the state or country, and after each item of an address (but not before or after the ZIP code).

Using Commas Correctly

Insert commas where necessary in the following sentences.

1. Dear Aunt Ruth

    We are having our annual Baylor Home Days parade next weekend. I hope you can join us.

    Your niece

    Cyndy

2. Kirsten asked "Who is the Grand Marshal of this year's parade?"

3. "Mr. Perkins who is the town pharmacist was chosen this year" Carlos answered "and I hear he is very pleased."

4. The parade begins at noon on July 15 which happens to be my birthday.

5. You'll be proud to say that you come from Baylor Ohio on July 15.

6. I know that parades are held all over the country during the summer but this one will be special to us.

7. Community organizations, which plan their floats for months, work feverishly on the night before the parade.

8. On the morning of the parade organizers meet early in the school gym.

9. They go over their plans and they double-check the parade route with the police department.

10. The best parade was on July 14 1995 when the Governor joined our celebration.

11. "Celebrating our heritage" Marty said "brings us all closer together."

12. Dear Cyndy

    Thanks for inviting me to your town parade. I had a wonderful time in Baylor Ohio and I would love to come back next year.

    Fondly

    Aunt Ruth

CHAPTER 11

For use with Pupil's Edition pp. 255–257

GRAMMAR, USAGE, AND MECHANICS WORKBOOK   **181**

More Commas

A. Using Commas Correctly

Add commas where necessary in the following sentences. If the sentence is correct, write **Correct** next to the sentence.

1. Senator Braun commented "The bill has a good chance of passing." _____

2. Maria overslept by an hour but she still made it to work on time. _____

3. The last time I saw Derek Jim and I heard him play the guitar. _____

4. We flew to Nashville Tennessee on January 25 1998 for the recital. _____

5. It was October 29 1929 that a terrible stock market crash occurred. _____

6. Steve's injury did not require surgery nor did he need physical therapy. _____

7. The animal that we saw in the woods was a muskrat. _____

8. "Well" the clerk replied "we don't have that item in stock right now." _____

9. My first bicycle which was a sporty red model will always hold a
   special place in my heart. _____

10. When the small fire started throughout the hospital alarms sounded. _____

11. Did Deborah resign from the organization or has she decided to stay? _____

12. James Buchanan was the only president who remained single. _____

13. The day before the airline had lowered its prices dramatically. _____

14. Curling which is played on ice probably began in Scotland. _____

15. The vise-grip which is a wrenchlike tool resembles pliers. _____

B. Using the Comma in a Dialogue

Add commas where they are necessary in the following dialogue.

"I love parades" said Marcia. "Don't you?"

"The Thanksgiving Day parade which is strangely enough always held on Thanksgiving morning is my favorite holiday tradition" agreed Kevin. "Call me old-fashioned but I enjoy the marching bands and I can't wait to see the clowns on unicycles."

"My favorites are the huge balloons that look like cartoon characters" Marcia said "and the floats filled with celebrities."

"It's almost time for the parade to begin and I'm ready for it" said Kevin. "If I don't get home by two o'clock which is the time Mom plans to serve dinner I will really be disappointed."

"Let the annual parade in New York City New York begin!" exclaimed Marcia.

More Commas

Application

A. Proofreading a Letter

Proofread the following letter for punctuation errors. Insert commas where
necessary.

Dear Kelly

    I thought you might like to know what I've been up to lately. This summer

has been great. Starting July 5 our church group participated in a social

service project. We traveled to Guatemala City Guatemala. There we helped

another church group which was from Topeka Kansas build a simple clinic.

We stayed there for about three weeks. If you know of anyone who might

want to contribute to the fund for the clinic, you can send a check to my

church at 3279 Oak Street Columbia WI 55555.

    Each week before church services volunteers assemble in the rectory.

We think about other service projects we can work on. I really like the people

I have worked with and I'm planning on returning to Guatemala next year.

Maybe you can join us.

Your friend

Bill

B. Writing with Commas

Write an imaginary conversation between two people walking into school this
morning. Include direct quotations and compound sentences. Also include at least
one nonessential clause and one essential clause. Be sure that you use commas
to avoid any reader confusion about your intended meaning. Remember to begin
a new paragraph every time you change speakers.

_____

_____

_____

_____

_____

_____

_____

CHAPTER 11

Semicolons and Colons

Lesson 4

Reteaching

A **semicolon** marks a break in a sentence; it is stronger than a comma, but not as strong as a period. Use a semicolon in the following ways: to join the parts of a compound sentence if no coordinating conjunction is used; to separate the parts of a series when there are commas within the parts; and before a conjunctive adverb that joins the clauses of a compound sentence.

> Twelve actresses tried out for the leading role in the musical; only three were called back for a second reading.

> The first was from Garfield, Pennsylvania; the second was from Waco, Texas; and the third was from Los Angeles, California.

> All 12 did well; however, the first and third auditioned best.

A **colon** indicates that a list, a quotation, or an explanation follows. Use a colon in the following ways: to introduce a list of items; between two independent clauses when the second explains or summarizes the first; and to introduce a long or formal quotation.

> The perfect actress for this role will have the following qualities: enthusiasm, the ability to dance well, and a strong singing voice.

> After the second audition the choice was clear: Melinda sang like an angel.

> William Shakespeare wrote: "All the world's a stage, and all the men and women merely players; they have their exits and entrances; and one man in his time plays many parts."

Also use a colon in these places: after the greeting of a business letter; between numerals indicating hours and minutes; and in references to religious works.

Using Semicolons and Colons

Add semicolons and colons appropriately to the following sentences.

1. Jim enjoys history, literature, and psychology but Rebecca prefers math, science, and music.
2. Beethoven visited Vienna in 1787 Mozart heard him play there.
3. Dan is interested in Japan consequently, he enjoyed the novel *Shogun*.
4. The runner has trained for months unfortunately, yesterday he broke his ankle.
5. Alison is a real gymnastics expert she has been participating in gymnastics for nine years.
6. Before you paint, gather the following things paint, a palette, and brushes.
7. Let's ask Sylvia to play the piano she's the best pianist I know.
8. The plane took off at exactly 5 28 P.M.
9. Rembrandt was a great painter nevertheless, he died penniless.
10. For skiing you need the following skis, poles, a warm jacket, a hat, and gloves.
11. In one of his essays, Ralph Waldo Emerson wrote "Though we travel the world over to find the beautiful, we must carry it with us or we find it not."
12. E. B. White was an essayist however, he is best known for the children's book *Charlotte's Web*.

(For use with Pupil's Edition pp. 258–259)

Lesson 4

Semicolons and Colons

More Practice

A. Using the Semicolon and the Colon

Add semicolons and colons where they are needed in the numbered sentences.

To jump-start a car in cold weather, first, find another car with a strong battery. **(1)** Then, take the following safety precautions make sure that the cars do not touch turn off the ignitions of both cars turn off all accessories in both cars.

Now, take a set of jumper cables coded with black and red markings. **(2)** Locate the positive terminals of the two batteries then connect the clamps of the red cable to the positive terminals. **(3)** Next, connect one clamp of the black cable to the negative terminal of the assisting battery connect the other clamp of the black cable to the engine block of the car to be started.

(4) When all the cables are connected, start the engine of the assisting car then start the engine of the other car. Once you have cut the engine of the assisting car, take one important final step for safety's sake. **(5)** Remove the cable clamps in the reverse order from the way you connected them first, disconnect one of the black cable's clamps from the engine block then, disconnect the other from the assisting battery and, finally, disconnect the red cable's clamps from the positive terminals.

B. Using the Semicolon and the Colon in Writing

Write the words from each sentence that should be followed by a semicolon or colon. Write the correct punctuation mark following the word. If the sentence is punctuated correctly, write **Correct**.

1. That play has been a great success it has played for several months to packed audiences.

_____

2. Critics approve of the treatment of all of these elements the theme, the acting, the writing, and the staging.

_____

3. Audiences enjoy the play's fast pace, its light humor, and its touching message.

_____

4. One theater critic wrote "Although at first I could not understand the motivations of all the characters, as the play progressed I found myself actually liking these misfits and hoping that their lives would finally work out."

_____

5. I did not reserve tickets to the play in advance consequently, I couldn't get any on the day of the show.

_____

6. I learned my lesson: always plan ahead.

_____

7. I saw my first professional play in Frankfort, Kentucky my second in Chicago, Illinois and my third in New York City, New York.

_____

CHAPTER 11

Semicolons and Colons

Application

A. Proofreading a Movie Review

The reporter who wrote this movie review was in a great hurry. She omitted both
semicolons and colons. Prepare her review for publishing by adding the needed
semicolons and colons. Then rewrite the article correctly.

> Kate is a big-city lawyer with a problem she can't seem to make any
> personal commitments. Rick is the super in her apartment building. Only in the
> world of movies can a couple like this one come together nevertheless, that is
> the premise that audiences are expected to swallow in this light, ultimately
> forgettable romance. Both actors do a creditable job Kate is likable in an odd,
> weak sort of way and Rick is attractive and sympathetic, although not very
> bright. If you have nothing better to do, go to see this movie. However, I can
> suggest a few alternatives wash the dishes, vacuum the rug, or read a book.

_____

_____

_____

_____

_____

_____

_____

B. Writing Sentences with Semicolons and Colons

For each item, write the sentence that is described in parentheses.

> **EXAMPLE** (sentence that uses a semicolon to join the parts of a compound
> sentence without a coordinating conjunction)
> *My sister is learning how to drive a car; she just got her
> learner's permit.*

1. (sentence that uses a colon to introduce a long quotation)

_____

_____

2. (sentence that uses a semicolon to separate parts when commas appear
within parts of a series)

_____

_____

3. (sentence that uses a colon to introduce a list of items)

_____

_____

For use with Pupil's Edition pp. 258–259

Quotation Marks

Reteaching

Quotation marks indicate that a statement by another person is being used word for word. Use quotation marks at the beginning and at the end of a direct quotation.

> "The mystery is solved," announced the detective.

Use single quotation marks when you write a quotation within a quotation.

> "The guilty party already admitted, 'I stole the money,' " said the private eye.

When a direct quote is divided by explanatory words, use quotation marks before and after each part of the quotation. If the second part of a divided quotation is a new sentence, use a capital letter.

If one speaker's words continue for more than a paragraph, begin each paragraph with a quotation mark. However, do not use the closing quotation mark until the end of the entire quotation.

In dialogue, whenever the speaker changes, begin a new paragraph and use a separate set of quotation marks.

Put a period or a comma ending a quotation inside the quotation marks. *Example:* "I enjoy mysteries," Gina said.

Put a quotation mark or exclamation inside the quotation marks if the quotation states a question or an exclamation. *Example:* "Who is your favorite author?" Matt asked.

Put a question mark or exclamation point outside quotation marks if the sentence states a question or the exclamatory remark contains a quotation. *Example:* Have you ever read the mystery story "The Gold Bug"?

Put a colon or a semicolon outside the closing quotation mark. *Example:* Sometimes private detectives are called "private eyes"; the word *eye* stands for *investigator.*

Use quotation marks to enclose the titles of magazine articles, chapters, short stories, TV episodes, essays, short poems, and songs.

Using Quotation Marks

Add quotation marks where necessary in each sentence or conversation.

1. Where is my diamond necklace? asked Mrs. Moneybags.

2. It must have been stolen! she wailed.

3. Let's call in a private detective, said her husband, to find the culprit.

4. Hello, my name is Sherlock Schwartz, said the private investigator.

   I'm so glad you have finally come. I was just frantic! said Mrs. Moneybags.

5. Mrs. Moneybags explained, Here's what happened. I had been entertaining my guests all day, and I know I had it on when they left. I might have set it down on the picnic table.

   What do you think might have happened to it, Mr. Schwartz?

6. Does this situation remind you of the story Diamonds in Jeopardy?

7. The detective explained, The great Sherlock Holmes once said, Once you eliminate the impossible, whatever is left, no matter how improbable, must be true.

Quotation Marks

More Practice

A. Writing Sentences with Quotation Marks

Add quotation marks, commas, and end marks where necessary in each sentence.
If the sentence is correct, write **Correct** on the line.

1. I'm sure you will enjoy J. D. Salinger's short stories said Ms. Phillips.   _____

2. I can't believe exclaimed Anita that motion pictures were invented in 1891   _____

3. Jennifer asked Why did John Donne say No man is an island   _____

4. A famous poem by Christina Rossetti begins, "Who has seen the wind?"   _____

5. When Neil Armstrong stepped onto the moon, he said That's one small step for a man, one giant leap for mankind.   _____

6. If I am elected the candidate declared I promise to cut your taxes   _____

7. I am just happy to have done my part the athlete said with a grin. Now it's time to celebrate!   _____

8. Let's meet back here in one hour, okay?

   No, I was hoping to explore this area for at least two hours.   _____

9. "If you look closely at this building you will see that it has many of the characteristics of the classic Georgian style. For example, see the absolutely symmetrical placement of doors and windows.

   This house, on the other hand, looks more like a Victorian.   _____

10. "When Thomas Paine wrote, 'These are the times that try men's souls,' he was trying to win support for the American Revolution," Keith explained.   _____

B. Using Quotation Marks

Add quotation marks where necessary.

Shortly after 2:00 A.M. on April 15, 1912, the ship *Titanic* slid to its watery grave. The passenger liner, on its maiden voyage from England to New York, had struck an iceberg in the North Atlantic.

William Ryan, a geologist at Columbia University, believes the *Titanic* can be salvaged. The only question, he says, is how much money you're willing to spend. We're talking about hundreds of millions of dollars.

A French team has already brought up such items as trays and dishes from the wreck. In a magazine article the team leader says, None of the items we brought up will be sold for profit.

Ruth Blanchard, a survivor of the *Titanic*, opposes plans to disturb it. It's the graveyard of 1,500 people, she says. I believe they should be left in peace.

For use with Pupil's Edition pp. 260–263

Quotation Marks

Application

A. Correcting Misuse of Quotation Marks

Rewrite the following sentences, using quotation marks, commas, and end marks correctly.

1. Cyndy says that "her favorite mystery writer is Derek Sullivan," the author of the short story 'Midnight in the Desert'.

_____

_____

2. What is causing the mysterious illness, asked Joseph, and who will be struck down next?

_____

_____

3. "The population is becoming "panicked,' or so the town mayor says explained Zack.

_____

_____

4. Run for your lives! shouted the town sheriff. There's a cloud of gas bearing down on us!

_____

_____

5. 'The story was made into a "television" episode called Desert Disease, said Cyndy. It's going to air tonight.'

_____

_____

B. Writing with Quotation Marks

Write a short dialogue that you might overhear outside a theater showing a mystery movie. Make sure that you indicate clearly who is speaking. Use quotation marks and other punctuation marks correctly.

_____

_____

_____

_____

_____

CHAPTER 11

Other Punctuation

Reteaching

Here are ways to use the hyphen, the apostrophe, the dash, and parentheses.

hyphens	apostrophes	dashes	parentheses
• when part of a word must be carried over from one line to the next • in compound numbers from twenty-one to ninety-nine • in fractions, for example, *one-half* • in certain compound nouns, such as, *about-face, ex-wife,* and *sci-fi* • between words that make up a compound adjective, such as *best-known,* when they precede the word modified	• with an *s* to form the possessive of nouns, for example, one *teacher's* desk or many *students'* tests • with an *s* to form the possessive of an indefinite pronoun, for example, *anybody's* • with an *s* to form the plurals of letters, numerals, and words used as words, such as *A's, 10's, no's* • to show the omission of numbers in a date, for example, *winter of '89* • in a contraction, such as *couldn't*	• to signal an abrupt change of thought or an idea that breaks into the flow of a sentence • after a series to indicate that a summary statement will follow	• to set off material that is loosely related to the sentence

A. Using the Hyphen and Parentheses

Add hyphens and parentheses where they are needed in the following sentences.

1. Some of the best loved stories from our childhood are folktales and fairy tales.
2. Whether you are five or ninety five, you enjoy a good story.
3. My favorite folktale you may like it, too is "The Three Sillies."
4. In that story if I remember it correctly a young girl is sent to fetch her brothers.
5. Along the way, she imagines her future a happy one with a husband and children.
6. In her daydream, she sees her son a handsome young man die in an accident.
7. Immediately can you believe it? she sits down and starts crying about an event that may never come to pass.
8. Later hours had passed, after all her parents begin to wonder where she is.
9. Soon talk about silly! her mother and her father find her and start sobbing, too.
10. They are three sillies crying about an imagined event that may never happen! Aren't we all guilty of this at one time or another?

B. Using the Apostrophe and the Dash

Add apostrophes and dashes where they are needed in these sentences.

1. The skaters movements her performance took ten minutes were slow and graceful.
2. All the players uniforms were muddy it had been raining all day.
3. I didnt know my ABCs until I was five years old that was in 92.
4. Karen, Tracy, and Laura these are the students who are planning the dance.
5. I dont need anybodys help right now.

For use with Pupil's Edition pp. 264–267

Other Punctuation

More Practice

A. Using the Apostrophe and the Dash Correctly

Rewrite each sentence, adding apostrophes and dashes where necessary.

1. Beatrix Potters book *The Tale of Peter Rabbit* has been a favorite with children
the world over don't you remember hearing it as a child?

_____

_____

2. In the story, Peter a mischievous bunny if there ever was one sneaks into
Mr. McGregors garden for a snack.

_____

_____

3. Peters jacket he was supposed to take good care of it becomes snagged on
the garden fence.

_____

_____

4. Its anybodys guess how many children have heard this story over the past
hundred years it must be quite a few.

_____

_____

B. Using Punctuation Marks Correctly

Decide if each of the following sentences is punctuated correctly. If so, write **Correct**
on the line. If it has punctuation errors, rewrite it, adding the appropriate punctuation.

1. The old house Mr. Evanss grandfather built lacks good plumbing, central heating,
and electricity some of the modern conveniences we take for granted.

_____

_____

2. Hal's business venture—a foray into retail sales over the Internet—was short-lived.

_____

_____

3. Almost two thirds of the people polled I was part of the group polled think that
the president elect is well-prepared for the position.

_____

_____

CHAPTER 11

Lesson 6

Other Punctuation

Application

A. Proofreading for Correct Punctuation

Add hyphens, apostrophes, dashes, and parentheses where necessary in the following paragraph.

"The Three Little Pigs" is a well known folktale beloved by children all over the world. Its characters are three little pigs who build a house of straw, a house of sticks, and a house of bricks a home for each of them. Ill bet youve heard this story before, right? The pig who built the house of bricks he was the smart one, remember? tells his brothers that their houses arent safe and that they should move in with him. They laugh at him big brothers are sometimes overprotective and happily live in their flimsy houses for a while, that is. When the big, bad wolf comes to call you knew this was coming he destroys the weak houses with a huff and a puff. But when the wolf reaches the oh so smart brothers house, he cant blow it down. The moral of the story always live in a brick house if a wolf is out to get you.

B. Writing with Correct Punctuation

Write a sentence that follows each given direction.

1. Write a sentence that requires a hyphen.

_____

_____

2. Write a sentence that requires dashes and at least one apostrophe.

_____

_____

3. Write a sentence that requires a hyphen and parentheses.

_____

_____

4. Write a sentence that requires a hyphen and dashes.

_____

_____

5. Write a sentence that requires an apostrophe and parentheses.

_____

_____

For use with Pupil's Edition pp. 264–267

Ellipses and Italics

Reteaching

Use an **ellipsis** (. . .) to indicate an omission of words or an idea that trails off. Use a fourth period if the ellipsis comes at the end of a sentence.

> I thought I wanted a job now, but . . . maybe I'll wait for summer.
> What cliff? I don't see any. . . .

Italic type in printed materials and underlining in handwriting have the same uses, as follows:

Use **italics** to set off letters, numbers, symbols, or words when referred to as words.

> The word *Mississippi* comes from the Algonquian words *Misi sipi* meaning "big river."

Use italics to set off foreign words or phrases, such as *laissez-faire*.

Use italics (or underlining) to set off titles of the following: books, newspapers, magazines, the titles of plays, movies, television series, epic poems, long musical compositions, and works of art.

Using Ellipses and Italics Correctly

Decide whether each sentence uses ellipses and italics correctly. If a sentence is missing italics, underline the words that should be italicized. If the ellipses have the incorrect number of dots, underline them. If the sentence is punctuated correctly, write **Correct** on the line.

1. I can't solve this problem; it's just . . . _____

2. Did you see the latest episode of Pardon My Dust on television last night? _____

3. Do you know what language the word *kumquat* comes from? _____

4. The crowd on the dock shouted, "Bon voyage!" as the big ship pulled away. _____

5. Leonardo da Vinci's *Mona Lisa* is on display in the Louvre in Paris. _____

6. William Sydney Porter wrote under the nom de plume, or pen name, of O. Henry. _____

7. Even though I know that sweet cereals are full of calories, I . . . . eat them anyway. _____

8. Our school drama department is putting on the play The Best Years of My Life. _____

9. The magazine I read most often, Teens Today, is known for its in-depth interviews. _____

10. Today is so hot . . . . I can't even think straight! _____

11. On the television series One of These Days the main character is an out-of-work actor. _____

12. The epic poem Beowulf tells of a brave warrior who kills the monster Grendel. _____

Ellipses and Italics

More Practice

A. Using Italics

In each sentence below, underline words that should be italicized but are not.
Write **Correct** on the line if the sentence is italicized correctly.

1. The French call enjoyment of life or zest for living joi de vivre.   _____

2. In his poem "Birches," Robert Frost describes what he likes about
   birch trees.   _____

3. Do you know the origins of the word chauvinist?   _____

4. Last year, our class read the novel To Kill a Mockingbird.   _____

5. The ambassador was adept at handling social situations and never
   made a faux pas at an official party.   _____

6. Do you subscribe to Fine Gardens of the World magazine?   _____

7. The phrase *tempus fugit* from Latin means "time flies."   _____

8. Jeannine hopes to get the lead role in the local theater's production
   of Our Town.   _____

B. Using Ellipses

You want to quote the following passage, but you have room for only four lines.
Read the passage and decide which words or phrases you can omit and still
maintain the sense of the paragraph. Rewrite your revised paragraph on the four
lines below. Use ellipses to show where you have omitted words.

Many people consider Mahatma Gandhi to be a hero of the highest order.
His philosophy was to meet injustice with firm resistance, but without hate
and anger. For example, when the British government in India declared that all
Indians must buy salt from the British, Gandhi objected. To protest what he
considered injustice, he began a march to the sea, where he would gather
salt for himself from the sea's bounty. British officials did not interfere with
this peaceful but illegal march, and soon Gandhi was joined by hundreds of
people and news of his protest traveled around the world. After a march of
241 miles, Gandhi reached the ocean and gathered salt. It was not until much
later that he was arrested for his defiance of British law. Gandhi's calm
persistence finally won out, and years later, India won the right to rule itself.

_____

_____

_____

_____

For use with Pupil's Edition pp. 268–269

Ellipses and Italics

Lesson 7

Application

A. Writing with Italics

After you read the following paragraph, rewrite it on the lines below. When you rewrite it, replace all the blank lines with titles that describe your own personal preferences. Be sure to underline the titles that should be in italics and put quotation marks around the ones that should be set off with quotation marks.

Sometimes you get to know a person most quickly by learning about his or her cultural preferences. So, here is the rundown on me. My favorite movie of all time is _____. If I could take one book with me on vacation, it would be _____. A short story that I remember well is _____. The television show that I hate to miss is _____. A play that I have enjoyed is called _____. If I have a few minutes to spare, I like to pick up this magazine: _____.

_____

_____

_____

_____

_____

_____

B. Using Ellipses in a Dialogue

You know that in an argument, people often fail to complete their ideas because they can't find the right words or are interrupted. Write a dialogue between two people who are engaged in an argument. Use ellipses at least five times in your dialogue.

_____

_____

_____

_____

_____

_____

_____

_____

CHAPTER 11